SPELLING
&
GRAMMAR

1 ALPHABET

ABCDEFGHIJKLMN OPQRSTUVWXYZ

These are all the letters used in the English language. The letters at the top of this page are known as capital letters; those at the bottom of the page are lower case letters.
Can you see the difference?

This means that every word you will ever learn will be made up from just these 26 letters. All you need to know is which letters to choose and the order to put them in!

To help you spell words, it is very useful to understand some simple rules of how words are formed.

abcdefghijklmn opqrstuvwxyz

There are two kinds of letters that make up the alphabet. These are <u>consonants</u> and <u>vowels</u>.

Most of the letters of the alphabet are consonants:

bcdfghjklm npqrstvwxz

Five letters are vowels:

a e i o u

The letter y can be both a consonant or a vowel.

It is usually a consonant if it comes at the beginning of a word and a vowel if it comes anywhere else.

A <u>noun</u> is a word that names someone or something.

Some nouns are called <u>proper nouns</u>. Proper nouns name specific people or places:

Catherine	England
London	Paul

<u>Common nouns</u> are the names given to more general things:

dog	house
fence	shop
knife	book

<u>Abstract nouns</u> refer to things which are not objects such as thoughts or feelings:

happiness	anger
loss	surprise
hurt	love

<u>Collective nouns</u> are the names given to groups of people or things:

flock	swarm
team	shoal

Nouns that refer to one person or thing are known as <u>singular nouns</u>:

one sandwich
one drink
one cake
one apple

When there is more than one person or thing, they are known as <u>collective nouns</u>:

two sandwiches
three drinks
four cakes
five apples

5 PLURALS

Plural means more than one:
    one dog but two dogs

Some nouns are made plural by just adding s:

hat	hats
coat	coats
pen	pens
pot	pots

Nouns ending in x, s, sh, ch and o add es to make the plural:

fox	foxes
crash	crashes
echo	echoes
watch	watches

A few nouns ending in o just add s to make the plural:

piano	pianos
video	videos

Nouns ending in consonants +y are made plural by dropping the y and adding ies:

baby	babies
city	cities
puppy	puppies
country	countries
factory	factories
daisy	daisies
fairy	fairies

Nouns ending in a vowel +y are made plural by simply adding s:

boy	boys
day	days
toy	toys
ray	rays
holiday	holidays
way	ways
tray	trays

7 VERBS

A verb is a word which tells us what a person or thing is doing.

A verb can also show when something happens by its ending:

Watch me play<u>ing</u> now.
I play<u>ed</u> with my toy yesterday.

A verb can also be turned into a noun (naming word) by adding a suffix:

call	call<u>er</u>	calling	called
play	play<u>er</u>	playing	played
jump	jump<u>er</u>	jumping	jumped
print	print<u>er</u>	printing	printed
cook	cook<u>er</u>	cooking	cooked
walk	walk<u>er</u>	walking	walked
farm	farm<u>er</u>	farming	farmed
clean	clean<u>er</u>	cleaning	cleaned

8 VERBS

Verbs ending in a silent <u>e</u> drop the <u>e</u> before adding <u>ing</u>:

hope	hoping
rake	raking
ride	riding
write	writing
make	making

For verbs ending in a vowel and a consonant, you must double the consonant before adding <u>ing</u>, <u>ed</u> or <u>er</u>:

trap	trapper	trapping	trapped
spot	spotter	spotting	spotted
shop	shopper	shopping	shopped
clap	clapper	clapping	clapped
rob	robber	robbing	robbed
plan	planner	planning	planned
clip	clipper	clipping	clipped
pot	potter	potting	potted

9 ADJECTIVES

Adjectives are <u>describing</u> words. They give more information about a noun:

This is a <u>boring</u> story.
It is a <u>colourful</u> picture.

<u>Possessive adjectives</u> explain to whom the object belongs:

I like <u>your</u> hairstyle.

<u>Numerical adjectives</u> show how many objects there are:

I have <u>three</u> goldfishes at home.

<u>Interrogative adjectives</u> are questions about the noun:

<u>Which</u> colour is your favourite?

10 ADJECTIVES

<u>Demonstrative adjectives</u> distinguish one thing from another:

I would like <u>that</u> dress, <u>those</u> trousers and <u>these</u> socks.

Adjectives can also be used to <u>compare</u> things.
These are special adjectives called <u>comparative</u> and <u>superlative</u> adjectives.

Comparative adjectives usually end in <u>er</u> and superlative adjectives usually end in <u>est</u>:

| lucky | luckier | luckiest |

Some exceptional adjectives do not follow this pattern:

good	better	best
bad	worse	worst
little	less	least
many	more	most

An <u>adverb</u> tells us more about a verb.

It describes when, how or where the action of the verb happens.

Many adverbs are formed from adjectives. Usually, <u>ly</u> is added onto the adjective.

careful	carefully
quick	quickly
rapid	rapidly
neat	neatly

If the adjective ends in <u>y</u>, then this must be changed into <u>i</u> before the <u>ly</u> is added:

happy	happily
noisy	noisily
grumpy	grumpily
ready	readily

<u>Pronouns</u> are used in place of nouns:

Laura ate a cake. <u>The cake</u> was the tastiest <u>Laura</u> had ever eaten.

Laura ate a cake. <u>It</u> was the tastiest <u>she</u> had ever eaten.

Just like nouns, pronouns can be <u>singular</u> or <u>plural</u> too.

<u>Subject pronouns</u> are used when the nouns they replace are the subjects of the sentence:

I	we
he, she, it	they

Similarly, <u>object pronouns</u> replace the sentence's object:

me	us
him, her, it	them

Many words are related to each other.

Simple words are called <u>root</u> words: e.g. <u>move</u>.

A <u>prefix</u> is a group of letters which is added to the beginning of the root: <u>re</u>move.

Many prefixes add information to a word:

anti	against	antibiotic
sub	below	submarine
bi	two	bicycle
mis	wrong	mistake
pre	before	preview

Some prefixes give a word the opposite meaning:

de	defrost
dis	disapprove
un	unfair
in	incorrect

A <u>suffix</u> is a group of words which is added to the end of the root word.

Adding a suffix can also change the meaning of the word.

Some suffixes form <u>nouns</u>, (see also pages 3 and 4).

er	singer
ist	artist
or	predictor
ness	happiness

Other suffixes form <u>adjectives</u>, (see also pages 9 and 10).

able	understandable
ous	nervous
ful	wonderful
y	funny

One suffix forms <u>adverbs</u>, (see also page 11).

ly	happily

Some <u>nouns</u> can be turned into <u>adjectives</u> by adding y:

fruit   fruity
cloud   cloudy

The y at the end of these words is pronounced '<u>ee</u>'.

Words that end in 'y' have their own rules for adding suffixes.

Root words that end in 'y' do not change when you add 'ing':

try   trying

Root words that end with a vowel followed by y need not change when a suffix is added:

play   player

Exceptions: some words change the 'y' to 'i' when a suffix is added:

day + ly   daily

Some consonants are doubled in a word, for example, **tt**, **dd**, **gg**:

bottle	little
ladder	sudden
digger	giggle

All double consonants make the same sound as the single letter:

tomorrow	hurry
message	press
puff	cliff

In some pairs of consonants, one of the letters is silent. This means you can't hear them when you say the word, for example, **mb**, **kn**, **gn**, **wr**:

comb	lamb
knee	know
gnat	gnome
write	wriggle

You may have noticed that many words share the same endings.

There are some word endings which are very common. Here are some examples:

- ion	station	notion
	position	ration
	motion	lotion
	invitation	nation
	sensation	elation
	celebration	invention

- ous	enormous	generous
	nervous	venomous
	famous	gracious
	poisonous	vivacious

- dge	dodge	wedge
	ridge	edge
	ledge	bridge
	hedge	dredge
	badge	fridge

18 WORD ENDINGS

- ng	hang	sing
	ring	gang
	bang	song
	wing	rung
	thing	gong

- tch	watch	batch
	snatch	dispatch
	latch	witch
	match	thatch
	patch	swatch
	hatch	hitch

- nce	fence	defence
	chance	science
	dance	pounce
	prince	dunce
	pence	once

There are many more just like these examples. Can you think of any others?

Do you remember the word endings section? All those words with the same endings were all pronounced the same.

But, there are some words with the same endings that are pronounced differently.

Take a look at these words:

plough	though
cough	enough

Even though they share the same endings, each word has its <u>ough</u> pronounced differently.

Here are some more <u>-ough</u> words. Try saying them out loud to learn the different pronunciations:

through	tough
although	dough

20 WORDS THAT SOUND THE SAME

There are some words that sound the same, although they are spelt differently.

Here are a few examples:

pair	pear
hear	here
for	four
two	too
know	no
stair	stare
toe	tow
weight	wait

These words are known as <u>homophones</u>.

Learn to spell each of these words and then practice putting them in sentences.

Can you think of any other differently spelt words that sound the same?

Sometimes when words are spoken or written they are <u>abbreviated</u>.

Abbreviated words are short forms of two words together.

When they are written, an <u>apostrophe</u> marks where the letter or letters have been left out.

Here are some examples:

do not	don't
I would	I'd
we are	we're
we have	we've
I will	I'll
that is	that's
I am	I'm
could not	couldn't
we would	we'd
you are	you're

There are <u>7 days</u> in the <u>week</u>:

> Sunday
> Monday
> Tuesday
> Wednesday
> Thursday
> Friday
> Saturday

It is important to remember that each of the days of the week must be spelt with a <u>capital letter</u>.

There are <u>12 months</u> in the <u>year</u> and these too must be spelt with a capital letter:

January	July
February	August
March	September
April	October
May	November
June	December

First published 2000 by Armadillo Books
An imprint of Bookmart Limited
Desford Road, Enderby
Leicester LE9 5AD
England

Copyright © 2000 Bookmart Limited

All rights reserved. No part of this
publication may be reproduced, stored in a
retrieval system or transmitted by any means,
electronic, mechanical, photocopying or
otherwise, without the permission
of the publisher.

ISBN 1-90046-649-X

Printed in Spain

NURSE IN

Nurse Tessa Maitland flies all the way to Santa Fé
and meets her sister's attractive doctor, Blair
Lachlan. But she finds it hard to tell if he strongly
dislikes her or is madly in love with her . . .

To Tom Humphreys and Ben Hazard, without whose friendship and hospitality this book could not have been written.

NURSE IN
NEW MEXICO

BY
CONSTANCE LEA

MILLS & BOON LIMITED
London · Sydney · Toronto

First published in Great Britain 1981
by Mills & Boon Limited, 15–16 Brook's Mews,
London W1A 1DR

© Constance Lea 1981

Australian copyright 1981
Philippine copyright 1981

ISBN 0 263 73571 0

All the characters in this book have no existence outside
the imagination of the Author, and have no relation
whatsoever to anyone bearing the same name or names.
They are not even distantly inspired by any individual
known or unknown to the Author, and all the incidents
are pure invention.

The text of this publication or any part thereof may not be
reproduced or transmitted in any form or by any means,
electronic or mechanical, including photocopying,
recording, storage in an information retrieval system,
or otherwise, without the written permission of the
publisher.

This book is sold subject to the condition that it shall not,
by way of trade or otherwise, be lent, resold, hired out or
otherwise circulated without the prior consent of the
publisher in any form of binding or cover other than that
in which it is published and without a similar condition
including this condition being imposed on the subsequent
purchaser.

Set in 10 on 10½ pt Times Roman

Photoset by Rowland Phototypesetting Ltd.,
Bury St Edmunds, Suffolk
Made and printed in Great Britain by
Richard Clay (The Chaucer Press) Ltd.,
Bungay, Suffolk

CHAPTER ONE

SWIFT as an eagle swooping on prey, the great silver jet bore down on the drome. Her nose pressed to the port-hole by her side, Tessa saw a sprawling city, rust-red fields, white concrete tracks rush up and expand to full size.

Engines screaming, the 707 touched down, settled to a lumbering run. Graceful in air, clumsy on land, the big machine was like a swan.

'ALBUQUERQUE.' Seeing the airport sign, she caught her breath. There it was, painted in letters a yard high, the exotic name her friends in England had found hard to believe, impossible to spell. New Mexico, she'd arrived!

Hands clasped, she gazed excitedly out. What had it to show, this gateway to the south-west? New York had presented tiers of glittering towers, Chicago a tapestry of railroads, Wichita a real live sheriff, complete with ten gallon hat, twin revolvers, a star of office badge. Well and truly, North America was living up to her movie-inspired expectations.

Hissing a long expiring whine, the jet shuddered to stillness, to abrupt silence. Passengers and crew began to surge about. Tessa glanced swiftly in her handbag mirror and made a final check. At Santa Fé Marigold would be meeting her, she must do justice to her beautiful chic elder sister. Assured that her brown hair hung neat and shiny to her shoulders, her lipstick was unsmudged, she unbuckled her safety-belt.

From across the gangway came the sound of a throat being purposely cleared, a simulated cough.

'You are aware, Ma'am, that you need to trans-ship here to get to Santa Fé?'

5

Surprised, she glanced towards the speaker. So at last he'd deigned to utter, the red-haired Adonis who'd boarded with her at La Guardia. He'd stayed mute for five long hours, nose buried in learned-looking journals.

She'd had time to reflect how oddly human beings behaved. Like sheep, this load of passengers had been herded into a mammoth metal tube. Shot miles high, they'd sat for almost half a day eating, drinking, dozing, side by side, without the exchange of a single word!

Only now, at point of departure, had the red-head spoken. Tall, slim, distinguished looking, he was already on his feet.

She inclined her head. 'Thank you, yes—I gathered as much. I have a change of airline, I believe?'

'That is correct—the "Zia" operates to Santa Fé. I'm booked with them, too. Care for me to show you where we go?'

'I'd be most grateful.' She smiled her relief. Accustomed to only short-haul European flights on package-tour holidays, she'd found the distance from London to New York, New York to Albuquerque, somewhat daunting. White blazer slung over blue linen suit, hand luggage gathered, she edged aft along the aisle, murmured her thanks to the cabin crew.

By the time she reached the mobile outer stairs, her guide had started down the metal steps. Following him, she noticed a slight droop to his left shoulder, an uneven beat to his feet. It was the kind of detail she'd been trained to watch for. Unusually, too, for someone who looked little more than thirty, his domed head showed a cap of pink skin, a balding patch.

He turned to wait for her when he reached the runway, auburn hair crimsoned in the afternoon sun. Warm air blasting up to meet her, Tessa smiled delightedly.

'September, and it's still this hot? And that sky—it's the bluest sky I've yet seen!'

Her escort grinned. 'The climate here's excellent, and Santa Fé goes one better—it's seldom too cold, or too hot.' Kind grey eyes flicked her a speculative glance.

'You are, I take it, from the UK?'

She grimaced. 'Guilty, I have to plead guilty! Does it show, that much?'

'Only in your voice. I caught the accent, when you ordered from the steward.'

They moved towards the terminal building. He walked, she observed, with a decided limp.

'This far west, we don't see too many of your country-folk,' he said, as they stepped out.

'You don't? Well, you do have at least one who's a permanent resident. My sister lives in Santa Fé. Her husband owns an art gallery there.'

She waved her free hand. 'Until she married, this was Marigold's scene—she was an air hostess. She and Ramon met when she was working the transatlantic run.'

She couldn't restrain a smile. 'Their romance sounds like a game of "Consequences". New Mexican boy meets English girl, they fall in love; he proposes, she accepts, they marry. And the consequence is that they expect their first child, first week of December.'

'Great, that's great!' The grey eyes twinkled. 'And little sister's flown all this way, to lend moral support?'

'To do more than that—I hope to lend a hand.' She wrinkled her nose. 'But how did you guess that Mari's the elder?'

'Easy! She's obviously had time to get around. Pardon me, but you don't look that old—to have embarked on a career, I mean.'

She blinked up at him. 'I don't? Then I have news for you—I'm a fully trained nurse. A very recent achieve-ment, I have to admit. And this trip is by way of a reward, for gaining state registration. Mother and Dad, bless their hearts, made it their treat. Running a village store, they find it difficult to get away, so they sent me over in their place. With Marigold being pregnant and so far from England, and none of us having seen her since her wedding two years ago, they get terribly worried. And there I was, footloose and free till next January, when I start my midder course . . .'

Her voice trailed. Why was she rabbiting in this way, and to a complete stranger? The man's easy manner encouraged confidences.

'I trust I'm not boring you with all this family chat?' she enquired nervously. 'After all that silence in the plane, it's refreshing to talk.'

He nodded. 'Know what you mean. Well, once you've inspected Santa Fé, you'll rush to reassure your folk. Sis couldn't have chosen a finer spot. Me, I'm from Boston, and there's no place like home, but New Mexico's fantastic. Last tour here I had myself a ball, made good friends.'

'This time round then, you'll have a head-start.'

Glancing sideways, she was surprised to see the freckled face cloud.

'It's been a while . . . much water has flowed along the Rio Grande. Things have changed . . .'

Fearing that she'd touched a painful memory, albeit unwittingly, Tessa hastily veered the conversation. Describing the gifts she'd brought with her for the expected child, she filled in the remaining yards to the terminal entrance.

Glazed doors slid silently apart and, stepping inside, Tessa looked admiringly about her.

'Is this an airport? It could be a cathedral!'

The building was new, vast, full of light. Walls and high-pitched rafters were the colour of ripe corn, the floor had a sheen of glass and stylised carvings of birds and animals, vividly enamelled, decorated pillars and beams.

'If this is a sample of New Mexico, I can't wait to see the rest!' she exclaimed.

He smiled. 'The State's full of beauty of every kind—ancient and modern, natural and designed. Head straight for that escalator—the main concourse is overhead.'

Together, they proceeded to the Zia booking booth and discovered their Santa Fé connection was due to depart. A black porter, huge and handsome, trundled their baggage outside, along to the take-off apron.

Engine whirring, a small aircraft stood waiting, cabin door gaping. Setting eyes on it Tessa stopped dead.

'We're never flying in that—that toy?' she gasped.

Her companion chortled. 'That's our kite, all right. Don't worry, these six-seaters may appear fragile after the big jets, but they're safe enough. If the weather cuts up rough, then they don't fly. Personally, I get a kick out of this kind of travelling and prefer it to any jumbo. Should you get nervous, just grab hold of my arm.'

Taking instant advantage of the invitation, she clung to him until safely seated with the three other passengers. At once, the burly pilot revved the engine to a roar and signalled chocks off. Rattling and whirring, the little plane hurtled along the runway and heaved itself from the ground.

Tessa immediately forgot all her qualms. The rhythm of the engine, the rush of air, the sensation of speed, carried her away, both physically and mentally. For the very first time she knew the real thrill of flying, of moving rapidly a short distance above the earth. They skimmed roofs, highways, fields as, gaining height, the plane zoomed into the azure sky.

From his cockpit the pilot boomed back that they were heading due north-east. Speaking slowly and distinctly, the man at Tessa's side managed to make himself heard above the engine noise. He fed her all kinds of facts and figures, items of history, and was, she suspected, seeking to allay any fears she had left. She wanted to ask him his name, but didn't wish to interrupt the fascinating flow. Watching the sunbeams dance on his auburn hair, she mentally nicknamed him 'Red'.

Warming to his task, 'Red' went on to point out the valley of the mighty Rio Grande; the Ortiz, Sandia, and Jemez mountain ranges. Describing how in turn the Indians, Spaniards, Mexicans and Americans had settled the territory, he informed her that though it was one of the biggest States, New Mexico had one of the smallest populations, with livestock outnumbering people. Here in the heart of the old south-west there were Indians still living in centuries-old pueblo and ghosts lingering on in mining-towns; here, there were villages where no language save Spanish was spoken, where a man lacking stetson and high boots was improperly dressed. New Mexico, he claimed, was another world, one known widely as the Land of Enchantment.

He nodded down at the earth racing by below. 'For more than twenty-five thousand years, man has walked these slopes, these plateaux, these valleys. Early man sought refuge here from his enemies, then nuclear man came to develop weapons against his foes, in security and in secrecy.'

He pointed. 'That-a-way, you can see Los Alamos, "Atomic City", created back in World War Two. Nowadays, resources there are being used for research into treatment of cancer—as a nurse, that'll interest you. A case of weapons being beaten into ploughshares, wouldn't you say?'

Tessa was listening, but her gaze was on the magnificent scenery. In wide belts the country beneath them was changing, from arid rust to aspen green to bronze gold. She felt a wild exhilaration, a heady sensation of freedom. This, she thought, is how a bird must feel in flight. Behind her lay her old life; ahead, lay a new world. Never before had she been so aware of the vastness of earth and sky, of space.

'You've come at the right time of year,' 'Red' was saying, 'In good time for the full glory of fall. Wait till you see the trees turn to flame. The country then is really something.'

'It's beyond belief now.' Wide-eyed with wonder, she sat clutching her seat. 'This clear light dazzles my eyes and I have to keep looking at those high peaks because they're so fantastic.'

'Red' smiled. 'The Indians have a belief that the mountains hold a mystical power and that to look up to them is to set one's sights high. Who knows, maybe you'll fall in love with New Mexico, become a lotus-eater and stay on? This State sure has a lot to offer.'

The plane slowly started to lose height. Tingling with excitement, she waited breathlessly for it to land.

Almost as soon as she climbed from the plane Tessa caught sight of her sister. Tall, golden-haired and still slender, she stood waving energetically from behind a barrier.

'That's Mari over there, in the tangerine trouser-suit,' Tessa pointed out to 'Red'. 'You'll see we're not a bit alike—she's the family looker.'

The airport being little more than a landing field, the few formalities were quickly concluded. Rushing to embrace her sister, Tessa was surprised to see tears shining in her violet eyes. Marigold had always been the independent, go-as-she-pleased, elder child. Outstandingly pretty, vivacious, friendly, she'd been thoroughly spoiled from birth. For as long as Tessa could remember, she had walked in her shadow.

Stubbing out a cigarette, Marigold cleared her throat.

'You had a good flight?' she enquired huskily. 'The stop-over in New York went well? You could have flown straight to Dallas/Fort Worth, of course.'

'What, and miss seeing Manhattan? Oh, Mari, it's marvellous to be here. You look fine, just fine.' Glowing with happiness, Tessa squeezed her sister's arm.

Marigold grimaced and patted her middle. 'You really think so? Even like this, carrying all before me? So far as I'm concerned, pregnancy's one big bore, from start to finish! Seriously, I'm considering starting a new society—one dedicated to shortening this long ghastly period of gestation. The S.S.P.G., I shall call it. Pity the poor female elephant! On doctor's orders, I'm not permitted to water-ski, play golf, or tennis; a gentle swim's as much as he allows. Booze, late nights, he frowns upon, and my smoking.' She sighed. 'It's an existence, not a life, let me tell you.'

She clicked her tongue. 'Come on! Your bags are checked through, the porter has them on a trolley, so why are we waiting?'

Glancing about her, Tessa was searching for 'Red'.

'The man who was with me—I want to thank him. From Albuquerque on he went out of his way to look after me.'

'The guy with ginger hair and a limp?' Marigold queried. 'You've missed your chance! He passed right behind you a minute or two ago, with the driver who was here to collect him. I chatted to the man while we were waiting—he was from Los Alamos.'

She looked searchingly at Tessa. 'Did you fancy him? Don't look so despairing—you could easily run into him in town sometime, though that LA lot do tend to be pretty self-contained.'

She linked her arm through her sister's. 'Oh, Tess, it's great having you here—I've been counting the weeks, the days. These last months, I've been feeling very jittery and terribly out of touch. SF's fantastic, but I could wish it were nearer UK.'

Tessa permitted herself an inward smile. Absence had certainly made this particular heart grow fonder! As a working girl Marigold's visits home had been few and far between. Now she was avid for news of parents, relatives, friends, village happenings.

Talking nineteen to the dozen they ambled to the car park. Stopping before a saxe-blue Mercedes, Marigold jangled her car keys.

'You like my coupé?' she asked.

Tessa blinked. The car was gleaming, showroom bright. 'I'll say!'

'It's mine, all mine,' Marigold went on, proudly unlocking the doors. 'Rae has a sedan going on three years old, but he likes me to have the latest, the best. He's a super husband.'

You've not changed, not one little bit, Tessa thought, as she got in. What Mari wanted, Mari had to have. Her taste was excellent, expensive. Watching her slide behind the wheel, fair curls bouncing, cheeks prettily flushed, she knew a fleeting envy. Beauty, personality, a loving partner who was well-to-do, a baby on the way, Marigold had the lot.

'I'm bursting to show you our apartment,' she was saying. 'First, though, I'll take you on a short run around the city, so you can see where you've landed. Tomorrow, we'll do a real exploration. One word of warning— be careful the first few days here, take things easy. We're seven thousand feet above sea level and one's body needs to adjust to the altitude.'

She turned on the ignition. 'Santa Fé next stop!'

Smoothly, evenly, the big car purred along the highway. Confidently, Marigold handled the luxury automobile. Looking on, Tessa was impressed. Their parents' mini-estate was the only car she'd ever driven, and that very seldom for it was little more than a month since she'd obtained a full licence.

At first, after the panoramic views from the plane the scenery disappointed her. The land lay flat like a saucer, ringed by hazed mountains. The grass on the roadside verges lay parched, brown as straw and garish sign-boards had been slotted into the intervening spaces. But Tessa's excitement returned as soon as they entered the royal city of St Francis, drove through narrow winding streets lined with pink adobe houses.

Wide-eyed, she gazed at pretty patios, graceful arches, gateways of intricate wrought-iron, louvred shutters.

'Why, this could be Spain!' she exclaimed.

Marigold smiled. 'That's not surprising as the Spaniards founded the city. They came here in 1610 and they left a splendid legacy.'

She turned the car into a tree-lined square.

'This is the central plaza. That building over the other side is the Palace of the Governors and was built the year they arrived. See the Indian traders squatting under the portico? That's handmade silver they're selling, spread on those red blankets.'

Tessa turned admiring eyes on the gracious palace. Long and low, the softly contoured walls lacked a single

sharp angle. Directing her gaze round the picturesque
shops and shady colonnades, she drew a deep breath.

'What a perfect place to live,' she murmured. 'This
old-world charm is so warm, so welcoming. I'd feel
half-way to heaven, living here. You must love it.'

'I do,' Marigold admitted. 'SF's a lovely, lazy little
place; life moves at an easy pace. No building rises above
four storeys, have you noticed? It's not permitted. That
way, surroundings get kept to human scale.'

'Small is beautiful!' Tessa quipped. 'Could we take a
stroll, do you think? I'm dying to peep through some of
those fancy gateways and peer along the little alleys.'

They parked the car and sauntered through brick-
paved lanes, inspecting smart boutiques and sleepy
cafés. Flowers, trees and shrubs were everywhere; roses
ran riot over apricot walls, vines trailed from pergolas.

Unhurriedly, the people of Santa Fé passed along the
pavements. Many, Tessa noticed, had Indian features,
dark complexions.

'We're a cosmopolitan community,' Marigold said. 'A
pleasant and a peaceful one. Now, I think we'll go along
De Vargas Street.'

They turned a corner and took a few paces. Abruptly,
Marigold came to a halt and tugged Tessa back.

'No, not this way!' she snapped. 'Quick, about face!
Hell, it's too late—I've been spotted.'

She lowered her voice and spoke out of the side of her
mouth. 'Here comes my doctor, and he's heading
straight for us! Now I'm for it—I'm supposed to rest in
the afternoons.'

The man striding towards them seemed seven feet tall
and a sand-colour all over, his clothes matching his deep
suntan. A beige shirt worn open at the neck toned with
slacks slung low round a narrow waist and cut tight over
narrow hips; a cravat, loosely tied, was the same shade
of brown as his high leather boots; a caramel stetson
crowned springy tawny curls. Hawk-like eyes glinting,
wide mouth set taut, he marched up to Marigold. As he
drew close, Tessa detected a slight twist in the aquiline

nose, the legacy of a long-mended break, and a white scar on his left cheek, the mark of a long-healed wound.

'Marigold Ruiz! What, may I enquire, are you doing in town? Didn't I order you a regular siesta?' The words were drawled, but the deep voice rang with authority. Tessa flinched for her sister.

A sideways glance, and she saw that she needn't have worried. Flashing a sweet smile, Marigold gazed calmly up into the angry amber eyes.

'Blair, as if I dare disobey *you*! Just this once, I cut my daily rest a trifle short, and only for a very pressing reason. I couldn't fail to go to the airport to meet my one and only sister, could I? An hour ago she flew in, all the way from England. Tessa, I'd like you to meet Blair. Dr Lachlan—Miss Maitland.' From the one to the other, she waved gracefully.

Tessa saw his broad brow crease and eyes widen with surprise as the doctor looked in her direction. His handsome head dipped in the slightest of bows.

'Pleased to make your acquaintance, Tessa Maitland.' His tone belying his words, he briefly gripped her fingers and turned his attention back to his patient.

'Get away home, put your feet up!' he commanded. 'Spare a thought for your baby! Today of all days you should be preserving your energy, saving it for your party this evening. It is, I suppose, in honour of your sister?'

A second time the deep-set eyes flicked to Tessa, narrowed, half-hooded. Hard they looked, hard with anger and cold, cruel almost. The sharp, searching scrutiny sent a shiver down her spine.

'Clever you!' Marigold murmured. 'Tessa's staying till after junior's born. I'm very lucky that she's here—Tess is a qualified nurse, so she'll take care of me.'

The well-marked brows arched. 'You think she can? I wish her joy.' Conveying doubt, the sensual lips curved down. 'For now, adios!'

A click of heels and he went stamping off, leaving Tessa staring after him.

'That man-mountain, is he really a doctor?' she queried. 'You could've fooled me? A cowhand, I'd have said, had I been asked.'

Marigold laughed, but her laugh was over-loud and betrayed that she'd been somewhat shaken. 'Well, there have been occasions when he appeared to prefer horses to people. Riding is his one hobby—he has been known to ride horseback to visit his patients.'

Tessa shrugged. 'A good idea, if it helps to improve his temper—riding's good for the liver.'

Marigold shot a reproachful look. 'Oh, come, Blair's not that bad! His trouble is that he doesn't care for women overmuch. Well past thirty, he should be married by now. His gynae and obstets specialities don't enhance the attraction of our sex, I imagine!'

She jerked a thumb. 'We'd better get back to the car—I'd not like to risk a second encounter.'

'At heart, Blair's a man's man,' she continued, as they retraced their steps. 'It's hard to believe, but he actually volunteered to serve in Vietnam and went out with a medical unit. That's where he collected that scar. He didn't have an easy time and when he got back he had problems. His doctor father died while he was abroad and the clinic he inherited was in a mess.'

She sighed. 'Even now, I gather things aren't too straightforward. He has a mother to look after—there are no brothers or sisters—and the old man's partner is still round his neck. Laz Sepulveda's a darling, but he's getting on and tends to let things ride. Actually, your cowhand has a considerable reputation in local medical circles, especially for females. He's bang up to date— took refreshers on leaving the army.'

Glad that she wasn't likely to become one of Dr Lachlan's patients, Tessa glanced the length of the street and glimpsed the tall, lean figure disappearing into the distance. That all-brown man, why was it she'd found him so disturbing? He'd broken in on the Santa Fé spell, and she felt piqued. A pity his manners didn't match the charm of his voice; the drawl still rang in her ears.

'What was it he said, about you needing to relax?' she asked.

Marigold flapped a nonchalant hand. 'Oh, he gets obsessive about blood pressure. With him doing my physicals, is it any wonder mine shoots up? All right, so you don't care for him, but I find him dishy.' She tugged at the collar of her cotton jacket. 'My, but it's warm, I'm dying for a cuppa. You are, too, I expect. See how English I still am?'

The streets they drove along to get to the Ruiz apartment were tree-lined but dusty and the bright sun dappled the road, shadowing the houses. Halting the car before a pair of high gates bearing the sign 'Los Arboles', Marigold tooted the horn. A uniformed man peered through the window of the adjacent lodge, carefully inspected both driver and vehicle, then waved them forward. Untouched by hand the gates swung wide.

'All done by electronic control,' Marigold explained, driving in. 'This condominium's one of the smartest in town, and we've a good security system. We have our own pool, club-house, tennis courts. I adore living here, but Rae's pushing for a house when the infant arrives. That'll mean moving farther out and I'll miss folk dropping by. This near town I can get a party going in half an hour.'

Tessa smiled. 'The same old Mari! You haven't changed one bit. The party tonight, what have you planned, exactly?'

'Oh, only a modest gathering to welcome you in—some friends, a few of the nearest neighbours. We ask them to avoid receiving complaints about any noise.'

Tessa raised her brows. 'Supposing I'd not arrived on time, if the plane had been delayed . . . ?'

'In that case we'd have arranged a second get-together, tomorrow or the next day. We have something on most evenings.'

The semi-circular drive curved round a paved garden. Set well back in spacious grounds and fronted by flower beds, 'Los Arboles' had the look of an exclusive country club. Drawing the Mercedes up beneath the high-pitched porch, Marigold handed the car keys to a porter in livery, requesting that he should carry in the luggage before parking the vehicle.

Whisked into a high-ceilinged lobby, Tessa registered tall green palms set in tubs, black and white marble tiles, a slender fountain splashing water into a rock-filled pool. From behind a gilt reception desk, a clerk politely greeted Marigold by name.

'This is a block of flats? It looks more like a five-star hotel,' Tessa remarked, on the way to the lift.

'So it should, for what it costs,' Marigold said, as she pressed a button.

By the time she was ushered into her sister's fourth floor home, Tessa was beyond surprise. She felt like Alice in Wonderland, the wonderland of 'Homes and Gardens', glossy mags. Everything looked perfect, pristine. Light in finish, Scandinavian in design, the furniture gleamed, glass sparkled. The walls were a textured beige, the floor honey-coloured, the long curtains filmy white.

A maid dressed in brown with a lacy apron and cap came tip-tapping across the marble tiles. Neither young nor old she had a comfortable figure, a friendly face, a muddy complexion, dark hair and eyes.

'Tessa, I'd like to introduce Mrs Sanchez, our house-keeper,' Marigold said. 'Wilma, this is my sister, Miss Maitland. These past few weeks, you must've grown tired of hearing her name. Wilma is my right hand, Tess; I couldn't exist without her. Just let me grab a ciggie then I'll show you your room.'

It was more a suite, having a lounge area set two steps down from the bedroom and a display unit dividing the two parts. Again, the beige and white decor prevailed, cushions and covers in tangerine providing a splash of colour. The connecting bathroom was luxuriously equipped.

'All this, for me? I have it all to myself?' Delighted, Tessa bounced up and down on the divan. 'Yonkers,

Mari, but you live in some style! A long way you've come, from our little flat above the shop. How Mother and Dad would love to see it—I've orders to take lots of snaps and send them. They said to tell you they'll be over, as soon as they can make it; if they could find a home here, I think they'd try to retire. Now, how about that rest you're supposed to be taking?'

Marigold blew a ring of cigarette smoke. 'All right, bossy-boots! First, though, I'll get Wilma to fix us that tea I promised. And it'd be as well if you had a lie down, too—don't forget the altitude. Tonight, we both need to shine. Around seven-thirty, the first guests'll arrive, and it could be midnight before the last ones depart.'

Tessa frowned. 'You'll be up that long? Won't you get overtired? I thought you had to go early to bed?'

'I do, more often than not. For heaven's sake, don't you start to nag—I get enough 'don'ts' from everyone else around. Expectant mums should be indulged, my ante-natal manual says! About dress—anything goes to-night. If you have something long, not too formal, that'd fit the bill. And if you're short of clothes feel free to inspect my wardrobe any time—our suite's next to this. If you want anything pressed, buzz Wilma on the house phone—the extension's by the bed.'

The next half-hour Tessa spent unpacking, putting her things away. Spread between the long line of white built-in closets, her possessions looked lost. Frequently she paused in her task to cross to the wide window and look at the view. Away to the north she could see the purple mountains and they drew her like a magnet.

Her suitcases emptied and stowed away, she swished through the short row of hangers seeking something to wear. Eventually her choice fell on an Indian muslin gown. Ankle-length, softly ruched at wrists and neck, paisley patterned in rust, blue and gold, the dress made her feel truly feminine and the colours high-lighted her two best points, a fine skin and clear blue eyes.

After a short rest she took a leisurely bath and relaxed in lilac scented foam. The bathroom had an unusual window for it was made of stained glass. Watching the gem-like prisms of light cast on the marble floor, the shimmering ruby, emerald, amethyst, sapphire shapes, she thought back to the shabby flat she'd shared with nurse friends in England. Would they ever credit such luxury, when she wrote of it?

She spent time and trouble in dressing, brushed her hair till it shone like a shampoo ad., applied a light make-up. Even so, her efforts left her dissatisfied and she let out a sigh on examining her mirror image.

There was no justice in the world, she told herself. How did it happen that the same two parents could produce a first daughter with blonde curls, eyes the colour of a dew-moist violet, a model girl figure—and a second girl with mousy hair who was a 'Miss Average'? Tessa had always been middling in every way—in looks, build, colouring, ability—and it was dead boring. Away from her sister, the difference didn't strike home; But now she was here, it sapped her confidence.

She gave herself a little shake, a reminder that but for Marigold she'd not be in Santa Fé, and invited to stay as long as she liked. She was there to enjoy herself, and enjoy herself she decidedly would

All the same, she didn't hurry to join the party. For some time after she heard the door-bell begin to chime she lingered by her window. Watching the rays of the westering sun turn the distant summits to tongues of fire, she thought of the man on the plane. Would she ever meet 'Red' again?

As soon as she estimated that a fair number of guests had arrived she slipped into the big lounge, hoping that her entrance would pass unnoticed. To her relief Marigold immediately came to her side, to her rescue. A vision in peach silk with a rose-embroidered over-top, she took her sister by the hand.

'You look lovely,' Tessa murmured. 'No-one'd know you for a lady-in-waiting; you don't show that you are one bit.'

'Thanks—thanks a lot,' Marigold whispered back.

'You've boosted my morale. Right now, that's something I need, and need badly. What d'you know—here we have a party on our hands and Rae's not back yet. That gallery of his takes too much of his time. I'm rapidly becoming an art shop widow. Men, I ask you! Let's collect drinks, then we'll circulate.'

Already the big room was buzzing with chatter. Conducting Tessa from group to group, Marigold charmingly introduced her. Always, there came a similar reaction—a polite greeting, a surprised glance. Not once but several times the same remark was uttered, 'You two, you really are sisters?' Soon the question began to bug Tessa. Why were siblings expected to be carbon copies, one of the other, considering the mixed bag of genes each child inherited?

Standing back, taking stock, she was impressed by the elegance of the guests, their proud bearing, their meticulous grooming. Outside a jeweller's she'd never set eyes on so much gold and silver, so many gems. Several of the people to whom she was introduced had fascinating Spanish names; some of the others Marigold described as 'Anglos'.

At one stage of the presentation tour Tessa experienced a tense moment. Ahead, a group suddenly divided, and the gap left a towering figure revealed. Tawny head tilted, Dr Lachlan stood engaged in conversation with an ash-blonde clad in slinky black. A smile transforming his austere features, a white tuxedo showing off his suntan, he looked a different man, friendly, relaxed.

Her heart missed a beat. You should smile more often, she thought. Seeing him, watching him, she decided he couldn't be a complete misogynist. All the same, she had absolutely no desire to meet the doctor again. Deftly, she steered Marigold in the opposite direction.

By the time Ramon Ruiz arrived, the party was in full swing. Profuse in apology he rushed to greet first his wife, then his sister-in-law. A head taller than Marigold and two years her senior, he was a thick-set man of distinguished appearance. As he'd done on their one previous meeting, his wedding trip to England, he put Tessa in mind of the 'Laughing Cavalier' with his curling mustachios and small neat beard. A print of the famous Franz Hals portrait had hung in the Maitland home, back in Sussex, all through her childhood. Could it, Tessa idly wondered, have had a formative effect on her lovely sister?

Whatever the reason for her choice of husband, it was one heartily approved by her entire family. Everybody had taken an instant liking to this descendant of a Spanish conquistador whose merry eyes reflected his habitual good humour, whose exquisite manners revealed his high-born breeding.

Catching Tessa by the arm, he led her to the bar set out on white-clothed trestle tables.

'May I say how charming you're looking? And not a day older, despite the addition of two years?'

He refilled her glass with ice-cold sangria. 'Mari, heaven be praised, has taken my late arrival with good grace—I'm horribly late and deserve to be in the doghouse. First, a customer detained me, and then I had to look in on my mother on the way home—an urgent matter, family business. She lives in the west wing of this apartment block, with my sister. They moved here when our estancia had to be sold, following the death of my father.'

'Does your stopping to visit mean they'll not be here tonight?' Tessa was disappointed. 'What a shame—I've been looking forward to meeting them.'

She saw the smile slide from her brother-in-law's face.

'Sadly, they can't be,' he said. 'It's not possible, not with Rosita the way she is.'

What was wrong Tessa wondered. What ailed his only sister?

'Now, who'd you like to meet?' he was asking. 'Or has Mari already introduced our one hundred most intimate friends?' His voice held an ironic note. 'Don't get me wrong,' he added quickly, putting out a hand to touch her arm. 'This party is something special, for a very special person.'

He lowered his voice. 'I can't tell you how pleased I am to see you here, that you've come over. Right now, I'm worried about Mari—she does tend to overdo things. Your arrival's a great relief. Could you try to get her to ease up a little, do you think? This baby we're expecting, it's very precious to us, and to my family. My being an only son, our children are the only chance of the Ruiz line being carried on. My mama gets worked up about the way Mari rushes around, now that she's pregnant.'

'I'll do what I can,' Tessa promised, and watched Ramon turn his gaze on his guests. He moved close.

'Don't look now,' he advised, 'but someone is watching you.'

'The Romeo with the olive skin, standing by the buffet?' Tessa enquired. 'Actually, I had noticed. That informal get-up, the plaid shirt and jeans, and those unusual features—he stands out a mile. Does he have foreign blood?'

Ramon chuckled. 'Here, what is foreign? In New Mexico, we have every kind. That's Tony Arretino, and he's one of our most promising younger painters. I've a particular interest in him as I'm promoting his work in my gallery. We've loaned him a studio, right behind it. For an artist, he's remarkably diffident. Ah, I see he's heading this way now; I had an idea he was mustering his courage.'

Half-turning, he greeted his protégé warmly. 'Good to see you, Tony. I'd like you to meet our house guest. Till New Year, I hope she'll be staying.' The introduction made, he slipped away.

There was an awkward pause, a void. Tessa observed the sturdy man toss back the mane of raven hair that hung straight to his shoulders, shift from foot to foot uneasily, circle the rim of his glass with a finger-tip. Why, he's shy, she thought, as shy as I am!

She sought an opening gambit. 'You're a painter?'

'Ramon told you?' He was staring hard. 'It's difficult to believe . . .'

'That I'm Mari's sister?' she broke in, her patience suddenly at an end. 'Oh, please, not you, too! Yes, it's true. A good fairy blessed our parents' first-born with beauty but forgot to pay a second call, when I came on the scene. The pretty Maitland girl, that's how Mari was known, and I as "the other one".'

His eyes on her face, Tony Arretino shook his head.

'There, I can't agree.' His voice was gentle, and he spoke slowly, with deliberation. 'Sure, Mrs Ruiz is as pretty as a girlie mag cover, but you, you have the kind of looks that'll last—a fine bone structure, large eyes. For quite a while I've been studying you, and an artist recognises beauty when he sees it. Sincerely, I'd like to paint your portrait. You've no need to hide behind those curtains of hair, Miss Maitland, or belittle your appearance. This earth needs a sun and a moon.'

She caught her breath. Had she heard right? Her ears, had they played her false? No-one had ever called her beautiful before, not even her fond parents. 'Tessa, call me Tessa,' she said softly. 'You're most kind . . .'

He narrowed his eyes. 'I say only what I mean, I never pretend. Your glass, would you like it refreshed?'

At the bar he poured more fruit-flavoured wine for her, a Coke for himself.

'Alcohol I try to eschew,' he said, as he tipped the foaming brown liquid into a tumbler. 'This is safer. I live alone, work alone, and painting's my whole life. When I'm permitted, I specialise in portraits of the Navajo, one of our main Indian tribes. Most of all, I like depicting them at their work, weaving, tending sheep, fashioning silver.'

He followed her gaze as it dropped to the heavy bracelet he wore, set with an outsize turquoise.

'Right, first time!' Smiling, he raised his wrist. 'Hereabouts, we men wear bangles, as well as the women. Ramon carries a stock of native ware in the craft shop he's recently added to the gallery; you must be sure to see it. But then, you've so much to take in, during your vacation.'

The level of noise in the room had risen, had started to deafen. He jerked his head towards the wall of windows. 'How about making for the balcony?' he mouthed.

Out in the mauve-grey dusk they gulped fresh air.

'That's much better,' he said, filling his lungs. 'Crowds I can't abide, and I hate being shut in. My country beginnings conditioned me, I guess.' Gazing over the darkened lawns, he went on to speak of New Mexico's manifold attractions. He described prehistoric cities, ancient forts, mountain lakes, high plateaux, mysterious valleys, rushing streams.

Listening, Tessa was conscious of mounting excitement; the teller was as thrilling as his tale. The low husky voice demanded attention, the coal-black eyes mesmerised, held the penetrating glint of gipsy-folk. This was a man of unusual quality, a man cast in an exotic mould. She was fascinated by him.

A gong boomed and supper was announced. Following the throng into the beige and white dining-room, they found the long table laden with ready-carved roasts set on silver plates, crystal bowls filled with tossed salad, tureens piled high with red kidney beans and golden corn, baskets of crisp garlic bread, potatoes in jackets. Plates heaped, they returned to the balcony, found seats. Over the meal they chatted non-stop, talked of art and architecture, compared notes on England and America. Explaining his name, Tony told of an Italian great-grandfather who'd journeyed from Tuscany to carve stone for the building of Santa Fé's cathedral, the Cathedral of St Francis.

Insisting that he should wait on her he brought wine, then rich chocolate dessert, objected strongly when she protested that she'd have to start dieting next day.

'Why?' he asked. 'Your figure—it's perfect.' Her day, her week, her vacation, was made!

Dinner over, Wilma cleared a square of floor in the big

living room and dancing began. Rapidly, the space became crowded, body was pressed to body, cheek to cheek. Enraptured, Tessa abandoned herself to the music, to the movement. The world forgotten, she closed her eyes and surrendered herself to Tony's tight hold.

All too soon, the melody faded and came to an end. In a dream, she glanced up over his shoulder. In one second flat she was back on earth. A few paces distant, Dr Lachlan was watching, amber eyes glinting, broad brow furrowed. The wide lips moved and murmured a comment to his blonde companion. Following his gaze, she looked Tessa up and down, drooped the corners of her mouth, gave a disparaging shrug.

Tessa went hot, then cold, conscious of marked disapproval. But why? So, she'd been 'sent' by the ambience, carried away, but what had that to do with the autocratic medic, or his supercilious friend? That wound on the doctor's cheek, could it have left a deeper, inner, scar?

Silent, she accompanied Tony back to the balcony.

'You tuckered?' he asked, concerned. 'Worn out after your long journey? Maybe you'd like to go off to bed?'

Her good humour returned. 'What, with all this racket going on? I'd never get to sleep.'

'Then how about our taking a walk round the grounds?—that'd be more restful. The service stairs, we can make our escape that way.'

Hand in hand they walked across moon-silvered lawns, strolled beneath the blue-black pines. The sound of revelry faded as they left the apartment block behind. There was peace in the big garden, cool air, a sweet scent.

Speaking seldom and then scarcely above a whisper, they quietly sauntered. Tessa knew a sublime content. A late bather sent out a flurry of splashes from the swimming-pool, some small nocturnal animal rustled the bushes.

A sudden engine roar made them jump and the noise

was followed by the sound of other cars revving up.

'Seems like the party's breaking,' Tony said. 'Come, let me get you back. Now you should have the chance of some shut-eye. If we follow the curve of the drive I might be lucky enough to spot a car that's going my way—I could use a lift. I don't drive, don't own an auto.'

'Then you don't live here in "Los Arboles?"' Tessa asked, surprised. 'I met so many guests who did, I concluded you must do, also.'

A grin widened his mouth. 'What me, a struggling artist? Thanks for the compliment, sweetie, but my accom's a little different—I've a studio cum pad converted from a stable, back of Ramon's gallery. If it weren't for his generosity, I'd still be holed up in an out-of-town shack. Drop by, when you call on Rae.'

He slipped an arm round her waist.

'Folk are flocking from the lobby,' he whispered, drawing her to him. 'How about saying our goodnight here, in the time honoured way?'

Tenderly, his lips touched her hair, her cheek. She felt a ripple of desire.

'Tess, you're a great girl,' he said softly. 'Usually, I get tongue-tied at socials, but tonight—tonight's been wonderful.' Warm, moist, longing, his mouth sought hers; her pulse raced.

Loud, the crunch came from nearby, the sound of a heavy foot descending from grass to gravel. Startled, they jerked apart. A deliberate cough rasped the air, a very tall figure bore down from the shadows.

'Mind if I play through, to reach my jalopy?'

There was no mistaking the arrogant drawl, the remarkable height.

'A good party, Tessa Maitland. My thanks. Have a good stay. You're already enjoying New Mexico, I see—and New Mexicans!'

Metal clinked on metal, a red door swung wide. Sliding into his sporty car the doctor raced the engine to life, crashed a gear, shot down the drive.

The moonlight dimmed, the air chilled, the night lost

some of its magic. Tony's farewell lacked the promised fervour.

'See you—very soon,' he promised.

Unobserved, Tessa crept to her room, undressed slowly.

What a day! What a fantastic day! From East to West, she'd crossed best part of the mighty US, seen sunlight on prairie, moonlight on mountains, fallen in love with delightful Santa Fé, met a man who intrigued her.

Never before had so much happened so quickly; never before had she experienced so many thrills in so short a space of time, met so many interesting people. 'Red', Tony, everybody had been charming, with one notable exception.

Why was it that one person, that haughty doctor, kept turning up, spoiling things? What caused Blair Lachlan to be so brusque and unfriendly? With all her heart, Tessa wished that her sister had chosen a more run-of-the-mill physician.

Determinedly, she set herself to banish all thought of him, to fix her mind on the exciting holiday ahead, to concentrate on Tony. No miserable medic was going to spoil her vacation of a lifetime, no matter how tall, how handsome.

Yet it was the mocking eyes, the lean scarred face, that swirled before her as she drifted into sleep.

CHAPTER TWO

THE sisters breakfasted late next morning out on the balcony, Marigold in a lilac negligée, Tessa in a blue gingham housecoat. Wilma had set a rattan table with poppy-decorated china and sparkling silver, made a trolley ready with percolator, toaster, breakfast foods, jugs of cream and orange juice, a basket of fruit.

'I think everyone had a good time last evening,' Marigold remarked, spooning cornflakes into a bowl.

'I did, for one,' Tessa said. 'What an enormous number of friends you have; some I didn't get to meet, even. That glam ash-blonde with your doctor, who was she?'

'Debra Petersen? She's Blair's "Girl Friday" at the Lachlan-Sepulveda clinic; the "LS" as it's known locally.'

'His girl-friend, also?' Tessa poured orange juice so forcefully that it splashed.

'Could be.' Marigold gave a lift of her shoulders. 'Certainly, *she* has something going for *him*, I'd say; she went through a divorce fairly recently. He recruited her from Dallas—why that distance, I ask myself. She must have something . . . I told him to bring a partner, and he brought her, but they came and went under separate steam, I noticed. To me, it's a mystery why Blair hasn't married long since—he's one of our most eligible bachelors.'

She flashed her sister a sidelong glance. 'It's hardly surprising you didn't finish making the rounds, the way you were being monopolised. Why, Tony Arretino hardly took his dark eyes off you, all evening. I've not seen him betray much interest before, in girls. That young man's highly talented. Rae maintains he could be world famous one of these fine days.'

'He's—different.' Carefully, Tessa spread toast with butter. 'He proved a mine of information on these parts.'

'So he should be, being true-brown New Mexican. All the same—Hell, the sun—it's shifting this way fast and blinding me. Wait while I push back my chair.'

Her long skirt parted as she rose, revealed her legs. Catching sight of them, Tessa frowned, leaned forward.

'Mari—your ankles! They look very swollen.'

Flopping back in her chair, Marigold quickly redraped her robe.

'So what? Stood a lot last night, didn't I?' She pouted. 'There's no necessity for you to start doing the Flo Nightingale—Blair keeps a hawk eye on me. Today, what'd you like to do. This morning, how about our taking a look at Rae's gallery—he's bursting to show it to you. After lunch, I suppose I'd better relax but you could take a swim, if you wished. Tonight, we have a dinner date with Rae's mother and sister—they live the other side of this apartment block, so we can go on foot.'

Tessa nodded. 'Rae did mention. Did I get the impression that there's something wrong with his sister?'

Marigold pursed her lips. 'Didn't I tell you, when we were home for the wedding? Ros can't walk. After Rae's dad died, some three years back, she took sick. No-one seems to know exactly what ailed her, but the illness was serious and it left her immobile.'

She sighed. 'It's quite heartbreaking. Ros is exactly your age—just twenty-two. Her mother devotes all her time to caring for her and that means two lives are being spoiled. Conchita's not much over fifty and still most attractive; by now, she might've remarried. More than once Laz Sepulveda—he's Blair's partner—has proposed, I gather, but she'll not consider the idea, not while Ros needs her.'

Tessa's interest had been aroused. 'You have no clue, as to the origin of the illness?'

'Not one! Nervous exhaustion was suspected, I believe, but it's puzzled everyone, including the many specialists called in, from far and wide. Ros eats well, sleeps well, but can't walk, and refuses to leave the apartment. As you can imagine, this makes things difficult all round for the family. As its head, Rae carries an additional burden for Ros and he are Con's only children.'

Her brow narrowed in concentration, Tessa stared down into the garden. A taproot had been touched in her memory. In her mind's eye she saw a hospital ward, a corner bed, a young, sensitive girl. That patient's circumstances had been strangely akin—there'd been the loss of a loved one, a subsequent illness, the loss of mobility. In her case, the incapacity had been preceded by the desertion of a much loved husband, due to housing difficulties. Disagreement and dispute had driven him from the over-crowded home of the wife's disapproving parents, where the couple had been obliged to begin their married life.

Concentrating, Tessa conjured up a second picture set a few months later. Vividly, she recalled visiting a department store and seeing that same patient behind the cosmetic counter. Recognising her erstwhile nurse, the salesgirl had delightedly related her later history. Her husband had returned to her, and so had the use of her legs! Happily, the reunited pair had found a flat.

'What a coincidence!' she exclaimed. 'I knew a case exactly similar! My second year of training, it must've been. There was this girl in Women's Med put down as NDK—'No Diagnosis Known'. And none ever was, so far as I remember, though she must've been with us sometime, or I'd not retain such a distinct impression. Eventually, it all came together—let me tell you.'

She did, and Marigold listened attentively, but at the end she shook her head.

'It's a delightful story, but it doesn't help much. In that instance, there was a living husband who could come back, aid the restoration, but if it was the death of Ros's dad that sparked off her difficulties, what can we do about that?'

She shivered. 'Let's quit this talk of illness and hospitals, it gives me the creeps. Strange, isn't it, how you revel in all things medical, and I have a near phobia?'

Tessa shrugged. 'Well, we're very different people, aren't we?'

'You can say that again!' Marigold smirked. 'Now I'm no longer employed by an airline, I can make a full confession. Every lift-off, I used to silently say a little prayer, "Please, don't let anyone be taken seriously ill. And if some poor passenger is stricken, let another hostess be on hand." Even though I'd been thoroughly trained in first aid I was scared stiff, though I imagine I'd have coped in an emergency. All right, so I'm a coward in that respect, but I can't help it. We all of us have some kind of fear, I guess. Care for some fruit to finish?'

She offered the basket. 'More coffee? Pass your cup.' Handing it back, she looked pleadingly at her sister. 'You will stay the entire course, won't you, Tessa? See me safely into motherhood? It's not that I don't want this baby—I'm longing for it—it's just that I'm scared stiff!'

Tessa gave her a fond smile. 'Of course I will—isn't that why I'm here? Till New Year when I'm booked to start midder, I'm all yours.'

Marigold's eyes searched her. 'You've no-one waiting, back home? No impatient swain?'

'Not even a patient one!' Tessa tossed back her hair. 'The last throw, he got away—flew off to make real money in Brussels.'

'A case of "cherchez la femme?"'

'A case of "femme" already found—another doctor on holiday. She had an advantage over me, could offer the possibility of joining him in a practice later on. Dave always did have a main-chance eye. Just now, I'm fancy free.'

Marigold turned down the corners of her mouth. 'So that's the way the cookie crumbled—I had wondered. Never mind, there are plenty more pebbles . . . in these parts, particularly. It's seldom one settles for the first, or even the second. Remember my pre-Rae meanderings?'

'Do I not?' Tessa jerked her head. The air-line men had swarmed round her pretty sister like bees round a honey-pot, while she'd considered herself fortunate to attract one male at a time.

Marigold flicked at toast crumbs with her table napkin.

'The parents, weren't they scared you might find a husband this side, stay on?'

Tessa grimaced. 'The idea never entered their dear greying heads—they don't consider me any great risk.'

'Then they must be getting short-sighted in their middle age.' Her violet eyes serious, Marigold studied her sister. 'One hundred per cent you've improved in looks, Tess, the last two years. As proof, witness the attention paid you last evening by Tony Arretino, though I'm not sure he's your type. Our artist scarcely took his eyes from your face—I watched you two dancing.'

As did somebody else, Tessa reflected. An image flashed before her, the image of a long lean face marked by a white line.

'That scar of Dr Lachlan's—you said he was wounded in Vietnam?'

A blink of surprise, and Marigold nodded. 'He was lucky to survive. His companions in the forward unit were all killed, so I've heard.'

She shuddered. 'Here we go again—this talk, it's not good for my inside. Now, if you don't want any more to eat or drink, how about our getting showered and dressed? The morning is flying.'

By the time they drove into Santa Fé the sun was high overhead. As on the previous day, the charm of the city, beautiful, Bellini-pink, overwhelmed Tessa. When they'd parked the car, she asked if they could take in the centra plaza on their way.

'This place has such a wonderful atmosphere,' she murmured, as they took a diagonal path beneath the trees. 'I feel completely at home, already.' Stopping, she gazed admiringly around.

'Oh, do come on,' Marigold urged. 'And let's keep in the shade. This warmth, it's too much, in my condition!'

Glancing sharply at her sister, Tessa noticed that her face was flushed, her forehead beaded with perspiration, though she wore only a smock dress of light cotton, a bra and pants, thin sandals. Comfortable in her navy polka-dot shirtwaister, Tessa felt concern for her sister. Was she as fit as she appeared to be? Poor darling, it couldn't be any fun carrying extra weight all in one spot, even if it didn't show too much.

To distract her, she asked how it was that the adobe buildings came by their gentle contours, and learned that the mud bricks were hand moulded, then sun dried. Cool in summer, warm in winter, they provided good insulation.

'Thousands of years, they've built this way here,' Marigold informed her. 'Which only goes to prove how clever they were, and that nothing is new, ever, in this strange old world. This is Rae's place, coming up now.'

Ochre-washed, quaint, the premises straddled a wide corner. Inside, the white-walled, black-beamed gallery was divided into sections by linen-covered screens. Appearing from his office, Ramon conducted them round.

'Here we have a popular line with the tourists,' he said, gesturing to a range of animal studies. 'These are Arretino's work. Wait till you see his portraits, though—they're something special.'

The room was large and airy, the paintings well spaced. In marked contrast the adjoining gift shop was crammed from floor to ceiling. Handwoven rugs, blankets, serapes draped the walls; baskets, hats, bags dangled from ropes and clothing from rails; the show-cases spilled over with jewellery of all kinds.

A veritable Aladdin's cave, it had a presiding genie, a

buxom, black-gowned bottle-blonde. Decked overall with samples of native silver and turquoise ware, chains at her neck and dangling over her bosom, bracelets from elbow to wrist, belts corseting her waist, she sent out a metallic shimmer, a blue-green glow, at every movement.

Tessa gazed in wonder at the walking display.

'She must be wearing a fortune!' she whispered to her sister. 'Does Rae have Securicor transport her, to and from work?'

Marigold giggled. 'Actually, I suspect he has her live in the strong-room!'

Gallery and shop surveyed, Ramon suggested a visit to Tony, and Tessa eagerly agreed. The studio lay across a cobbled yard, and the top half of the plank door hung open. It revealed a topsy-turvy interior, a confusion of canvases and equipment.

In answer to Ramon's call, Tony came to meet them, a shy smile on his swarthy face. Wearing an oatmeal smock over blue jeans, he looked a typical artist. Lighting on Tessa, his coal-black eyes gleamed with delight and she knew a tingle of pleasure.

With modest charm, he welcomed in his visitors and, at Ramon's prompting, he bashfully produced one of his Navajo portraits for them to see. Immediately, Tessa forgot the surrounding disorder, for the face staring from the canvas captured her entire attention. Soulfully, the piercing Indian eyes gazed out on the world; the brown temples seemed to pulse with life, the long nostrils to breathe, the chiselled lips to move.

She caught her breath. How marvellous, to possess such talent, to have the ability to capture character in paint; every stroke of the brush had gone to create a masterpiece. Silent, she stood in admiration.

Tony came quietly to her side. 'You approve? You like my work?' he asked hesitantly. 'If you do, I'd be glad to paint your portrait, like I said.'

'You would? You really would? I'd make a good enough subject?' Excited, she clapped her hands. Such an offer, she'd never contemplated receiving one like it. 'Oh, I'd love you to—but payment, how much . . . ?'

'My pleasure,' he broke in. 'It would be my pleasure. Money'd not enter into the matter.'

Quickly, Ramon stepped forward. 'The sittings, you're certain you could fit them in? Our pre-Christmas show, don't forget we have that coming up, and there's the stock order. Time is of the essence—maybe we'd better wait.'

'But this can't—Tessa's vacation, she has only three months.' Chin jutting obstinately, body stiff, Tony fixed his gaze on Ramon.

There was a silence, a tense pause. It was Marigold who broke it.

'But Rae, couldn't this open up a new market among Santa Féans?' Soothingly, she stroked her husband's arm. 'So far, Tony's been restricted to studies of native people and local fauna, but if he does Tessa's picture and you exhibit it, well, it might easily start a trend. There's plenty of money around here, and people have big enough homes to hang their portraits.'

She flashed one of her brilliant smiles at the artist. 'Later, I'd like you to do my picture for me.'

Impatiently, her husband waved a hand towards the courtyard.

'Much later, next year maybe . . . Right now, I have to get back to my office.'

Bidding his guests goodbye, Tony let his fingers linger on Tessa's. The touch gave her a pins-and-needles tingle.

'That date, I'll be calling you,' he whispered.

At the entrance to the gallery, Marigold pecked Ramon's cheek. 'Darling, please try not to be late home this evening. It is your mother we're visiting, remember.'

'Tonight could be slow-going,' she warned Tessa, as they wandered back to the car. 'Laz Sepulveda's to be the other guest—he's Blair Lachlan's partner. Sep's a dear but a bit "set in aspic", a bit old-fashioned. He's

Conchita's "steady". She's a stylish lady, so we'd better don our longs.'

Chic, short, deep-bosomed, Ramon's mother made a considerable impression upon Tessa. At one and the same time, she managed to look kind but shrewd, friendly but firm—a typical matriarch, Tessa guessed. Plump hands extended in welcome, she came bustling to meet the three of them. Clad in crimson lace, dark hair elegantly french-pleated, diamonds glittering, she was as colourful as a rubra rose, as proud as a peahen.

Taffeta underskirt rustling, Chanel perfume wafting, she ushered them into a magnolia drawing-room bursting with gilt-legged furniture. At their entrance two figures moved; a pretty brunette waved from a wheelchair, a portly man puffed to his feet from a brocade covered couch. Graciously, Conchita Ruiz introduced Tessa to her daughter and to her doctor, directed everyone to seats and deputed Ramon to serve drinks.

Placed next to Rosita, Tessa was able to closely observe the invalid. A little more colour in her cheeks, rather less flesh on her body, and she'd be a beauty. Ramon's sister was his feminine counterpart. But in her hazel eyes Tessa detected a look of resignation, the resignation of the long-term sufferer, and in her low voice a note of weariness. Her heart went out to her contemporary. What a ghastly tragedy, to be confined to a wheelchair, while still so young.

The dinner, served in a chandeliered dining-room, was superb. There was shrimp and avocado cocktail, a tender sirloin, fresh vegetables, a bombe surprise; fine Californian wines accompanied each course. Though the hostess complained about being reduced to a staff of one, there was no delay in the service, the mistress keeping an eagle eye on the servant and Ramon acting as butler. Conversation tended to dwell on the coming child, Conchita making no secret of the joy she felt at being an expectant grandmother.

Coffee and liqueurs were taken in the drawing-room,

cigarettes and cigars passed round. Only Marigold and
Laz Sepulveda smoked, and Tessa noticed Mrs Ruiz dart
a reproving glance at her daughter-in-law. Watching the
rotund little medical man cough his way through a
second cheroot and swallow a third glass of cognac,
Tessa put him down as a 'Do as I tell you, not as I do',
type of doctor.

As the evening progressed, Rosita grew more talkative, more animated. Becoming interested in Tessa's
background, she asked questions about England, wistfully mentioning that a planned trip to Europe had had
to be cancelled, because of her father's fatal illness.

Keenly, the mother watched the daughter. When the
time came to leave, Conchita pressed an open invitation
on Tessa. Any time, she was to feel free to visit for her
company would be good for Rosita.

Her interest thoroughly aroused, Tessa quizzed
Ramon about his sister during their short homeward
walk. What did he know about her illness?

'Personally, I'm convinced it stemmed from the shock
of losing papa,' he said. 'Though even before that, she
wasn't really fit. I remember thinking how withdrawn
she was when I was summoned back from Europe because of father's physical deterioration. For over two
years I'd been away, working for fine art dealers. Rosita,
being the only daughter, was very close to papa and not a
little spoiled; she took his demise badly. One thing I can
assure you—no stone has been left unturned, no ex-
pense spared, in our efforts to get her better. Even a
pilgrimage to the shrine at Chimayo was tried.'

He sighed. 'It would be a miracle, an answer to all our
prayers, if she could be cured. Many problems, that
would ease . . .'

For some time before retiring, Tessa sat by her
bedroom window. Gazing up at the moon-whitened
mountains, she thought of Rosita, of how much her
history had in common with the English salesgirl. In
both cases, the afflicted were young, sensitive girls
who'd been cherished and adored. Of an age, they'd

each suffered trauma and in each instance the incapacity appeared of hysteric origin.

There was one differing factor. The English girl had had no home of her own, disputatious relatives. The desertion of the husband she'd loved obsessively had left her utterly bereft, devoid of interest in life. Rosita was infinitely more fortunate. In addition to a devoted family, she enjoyed security, luxury, every comfort. Pretty, intelligent, sophisticated, she had many blessings, much to live for. And she'd given the impression of someone with a determined will, a strong character. Tragic though the loss of her father had undoubtedly been, was it the real cause, the only cause, of her trouble? The obvious explanation wasn't necessarily the correct one, Tessa had learned, during her years of nursing.

It was all very intriguing, very puzzling. For more than three years, Rosita hadn't walked. Remember all she herself had done in that space of time—how she'd achieved professional status, independence, how she'd enjoyed holidays, games, swimming, parties, Tessa deeply pitied her. She should he having similar opportunities, she should be revelling in the good things the world had to offer. Instead, Rosita was chair and bed bound of necessity, house-bound by choice.

Determining to do all she could to help her, Tessa made ready for bed. It was her duty to hold out a helping hand, for fate had treated her extremely kindly. And it would be a way of offering thanks for her trip to Santa Fé, for her fantastic holiday, for the fabulous folk she was meeting.

Thinking of Tony Arretino, his dark exotic looks, his gipsy eyes, his hungry lips, she felt an excited stirring. How long before he telephoned? She couldn't wait to hear from him.

Next morning he rang, and the sound of his lazy voice sent her heart soaring.

'Are you free tonight?' he asked. 'Then how about a modest supper? Eight o'clock, would that suit? Okay,

I'll be round to collect you—watch out for a yellow cab.'

Well before the hour, Tessa was waiting in the lobby. Eight o'clock came, but there was no sign of Tony. Expecting him to arrive any second, she stood by the door and watched the electronic clock in 'Reception' blue-flash away the minutes. Five, ten, fifteen, twenty; she grew anxious.

What could have happened? Was he unwell? Could he have met with an accident? Nervously, she paced up and down, peered out into the gathering dusk, smoothed down her hyacinth-blue dress, re-draped the matching shawl. Till the half-hour she'd wait, no longer. The figures on the clock jerked on through the twenties; her spirits steadily sank. Had she been stood up?

'Three zero' flicked, and a cab came racing up the drive. Even before the wheels ceased to turn Tony was out, pounding along beside it. A flush on his face, guilt shadowing his eyes, he rushed to grab her hands.

'Sweetie, how can I face you?' he gasped out. 'All day, I've been longing for evening to come, counting the chimes from the gallery clock. Late afternoon, I got stuck into a picture and simply didn't hear. When I'm painting I get that engrossed . . .'

She stared with rounded eyes. 'You mean, you don't have a clock, a watch, of your own?'

He looked dumbfounded. 'What for? I'm no wage-slave, no city commuter, I plan my own schedule. The sun's my timepiece—dawn tells me that the day's beginning, dusk that it's about to end. Only occasions such as this find me at a loss, but in future I promise to do better.'

He looked at her longingly, so longingly she had to forgive his lateness, overwhelmed as she was with relief, relief that nothing untoward had befallen him.

'You look wonderful, Tessa.' Holding her at arm's length, he stared in admiration. 'That dress, it goes with your eyes. Now, let's get started—that cab meter's ticking over.'

'"The Freight Train,"' he directed the driver, when

they were seated. 'It's okay, honey, we're not taking a trip.' Reassuringly, he patted her hand. 'The FT's an eating place by the railroad. They serve the best barbecued ribs in town. While you're over here you'll get fancy food galore; this is genuine American.'

The timber building was strictly functional, outside and in. The floor lacked a carpet, the chairs and tables were rustic, the lighting basic, but a great welcoming glow came from the far end of the dining-room, the glow of red-hot coals.

'First, come and inspect the kitchen,' Tony invited, and led her to an enormous plate-glass window. Through it Tessa beheld a waist-high line of thick iron bars set over burning charcoal, long ribs resting in rows. She felt the blast of fierce heat, heard the hiss of sizzling fat, smelt the savoury aroma of roasting. The sight made her mouth water, but all that meat . . .

'Those portions, the size!' she exclaimed. 'Do you still graze mammoths?'

He laughed, and his laugh was gurgling, infectious. 'Buffalo, sweetheart. Don't worry your pretty head— eat as much, or as little, as you wish. Jacket potatoes to accompany, a green salad—does that grab you? That table in the corner—let's make for it.'

Settled, she nodded towards the barred window.

'Sitting here, I can almost hear the covered wagons, the rolling wheels, the neigh of horses, the crack of whips. A whole century, I've slid back.'

He covered her hand with his. 'For me, this present one's good enough: for me, life's just beginning.'

Despite the protest she raised on receiving her helping, Tessa tucked manfully into it. The meat devoured, she tackled the bones with gusto, following Tony's example. Smacking lips, licking fingers, they consumed every morsel. Mopping gravy from their chins, they giggled like children.

The music started up as they were finishing their jumbo ices. Seating himself at the ancient grand, a bearded man embarked on a 'Hello, Dolly' chorus; in no time he had the battered instrument edged with singers. Joining their number Tessa and Tony added their voices. One of the crowd began to beat out the rhythm on the piano top; others followed suit.

With incredible suddenness it happened. One moment the grand stood firm, the next it was wobbling. Positioned at the apex Tessa saw it slope towards her.

'Look out!' There was a warning shout. 'That mended leg, it's giving way!'

Before she could think, before she could move, the heavy bulk lurched at her. In the nick of time strong hands gripped her waist, swung her back. There was a deafening thud, a jangle of chords, and the piano nose-dived to the floor, lay like a sea-wrecked monster.

There was a strained silence. Nervous, high-pitched, a strangled laugh shattered the quiet, eased the tension. Everyone started to talk and move at the same time. Anxiously people enquired of Tessa if she was all right.

Breathless with relief she nuzzled against Tony, who still held her tight, murmured her gratitude. Shivering, she nodded down at the splintered wood.

'But for you, that lot would've landed on my feet!'

He blushed. 'That, I beg leave to doubt,' His mouth twitched into a fond smile. 'Anyway, I only acted in my own interests; it'd be distressing for me, to have you hurt.'

His lips touched her cheek. 'It's a devastating effect that you have! Even an elderly grand sinks down on its knees!'

He retained his hold, as if fearing to let her go. All the way home in the cab, he kept a firm arm around her.

'On an important date like this, there's a bonus in not being able to drive,' he murmured. 'I don't have to keep my hands on the wheel! With all that went on back there, I didn't get a chance to tell you how fantastic you looked, with the firelight in your hair. You don't have to envy your sister, not one little bit; your type of beauty is the one I prefer.'

She felt a long quiver of delight. Beauty, didn't it lie in
the eyes of the beholder? Here was a man who saw her as
she'd longed to be seen. Handsome, he was easy to be
with, quick-witted, resourceful, possessed a sense of
humour.

The cab drew up outside 'Los Arboles'. At first tenta-
tive, his kiss grew ardent, passionate. She felt a quickening of blood, a fervent stirring.

Breathless, he reluctantly released her, led her into
the lobby.

'Keep all the hours you can spare for me,' he begged.
'I can't see you often enough. Already, the thought of
you quitting Santa Fé, going back to UK, is unbearable. I
can only live in hope. Your vacation has only just begun
and, by the end, you may change your mind . . .'

He lifted her hand to his lips. 'Tonight's been
fantastic—promise you'll dream of me? I'll be calling
you, very soon.' Eyes filled with adoration, he handed
her into the lift.

Her heart sang, all the way up to the apartment. What
fun life was, in the Land of Enchantment; Tony was
super. Did her future, like her sister's, lie in New
Mexico?

Marigold seemed on edge next morning.

'My check-up's due this afternoon, I've to go to the
clinic,' she announced. 'I know it's routine, but I dread it
all the same. You will come with me, won't you, Tess?
The appointment's at four o'clock—Blair planned it
post-siesta.'

Though mention of the doctor's name jolted Tessa,
she was relieved to hear the news. At first sight, her
sister had appeared in perfect health, but closer observation had revealed that her hands, as well as her ankles,
were swollen; she couldn't remove her gold wedding-
ring because of the flesh that tight-banded it. Her eyes
were shadowed, and Tessa had discovered that her
radiant glow owed more to cosmetics than approaching

motherhood. In addition, she'd complained of suffering frequent headaches and was noticeably restless. It could be that the doctor would consider a protein and salt-reduced diet necessary, Tessa thought.

They drove into town in good time and she had ample chance to admire gardens bright with roses and calendulas, dahlias and petunias. Almost anything and everything could be grown on the soil, provided there was sufficient water, she learned from Marigold. Wells and irrigation ditches were used, to help out the low rainfall.

'And the weather here could stay warm and dry till November, apart from the odd storm,' Marigold informed her, as she turned the long-bodied Mercedes between high gates. 'This is it, this is the LS.'

Set well back from the road, the clinic was housed in a rambling colonial-style building. Outside, it looked early twentieth century, inside it was brand spanking new, spotless, gleaming.

'Blair had it all done over recently,' Marigold said, as they entered the vestibule. 'He's a perfectionist—everything must be just right for his patients. First, I need to check in with his secretary.'

In answer to her rap on an office door Debra Petersen came out to greet them. After showing them to seats, she took a few details from Marigold. Wearing an almond-green coat-dress she looked cool, elegant. Watching her, Tessa wondered what it was about her that she found so off-putting. There were few people she actively disliked and she couldn't remember feeling such an instinctive antipathy to anyone. Apart from that one glance of disdain and disapproval at the party, she had nothing against the woman. It was as a woman she saw her now, not as a girl, a woman of around thirty. The clear New Mexican light shining in through the big windows showed up the lines round the ash-blonde's green eyes, the firm folds running from nose to mouth. Her eyes gave the clue! They were hard and calculating and there was a determined set to her thin lips, a jut to her small jaw.

Promptly at the appointed hour a white-clad, white-capped, white-shod nurse appeared to escort Marigold into Blair Lachlan's office. Checking the long line of initials after his name on the door, Tessa was impressed by the numerous degrees and diplomas: even for Marigold, he should be good enough.

The magazines neatly fanned on the low table were current editions, glossy, clean. Flicking through the shiny pages she inspected photographs of film and TV stars, Beverly Hills homes, social gatherings. Three periodicals she perused, before glancing at her watch. For a routine check-up, Dr Lachlan was certainly taking his time. What was going on?

Uneasy, she got to her feet, strolled up and down, edged nearer his door. At her approach it swung wide and Marigold came hurrying out. Her face looked strained.

She caught at Tessa's arm. 'What do you think?' she cried. 'Blair has ordered me to be admitted here at once! It's my blood pressure—it's shot up, he says, and I'm to be kept in bed! Imagine that! Me, in this place, restricted . . . If I don't come in he says there could be complications, danger even, to me and my ba-by . . .' Her voice faltered. 'I'm not to go home, not even to collect my things . . .'

Her words faded, tears filled her eyes. Tessa threw out her arms, cuddled her sister.

'Darling, I know how you must feel. This shock . . . but if it's for the best . . .'

'You c-can't believe th-that! Why, it c-could be a three-month s-sentence. I'll be sh-shut in, all that t-time!'

A look of horror in her eyes, she stared round like a frightened child. 'Oh, Tess, I c-can't bear the thought, you know how scared I am of h-hospitals.' She clutched at her sister.

'There, there,' Tessa murmured, stroking the blonde curls. 'Try not to upset yourself—it won't do you any good.' It was strange the way she'd always found herself protecting her sister, though her junior by two years. 'You're sure that you got it right, that this is what Dr Lachlan meant? It's not simply a question of staying here till your bp comes down? He didn't mention . . .'

'Oh, stop, please stop! My head's going round!' Covering her eyes with her palms, she sank down on a chair and burst into loud sobs.

'I c-can't bear the th-thought,' she gasped. 'It's s-surely not nec-essary? Why c-can't I stay in b-bed at home, if that's all th-there is to it? You'd l-look after me, w-wouldn't you?'

She looked up mournfully, pleadingly. 'Oh, Tess, don't just st-and there—d-do something! Go in and s-see Blair, re-mind him you are a n-nurse, tell him you'll c-carry out any treatment . . . That way, I'll g-get better m-more quickly, I know I w-will. And wh-what's good for m-me'll be g-good for my baby.' She tried to brush away her tears.

Tessa bit her lip. 'Mari, I don't feel too hopeful. Doctors don't appreciate having their instructions queried . . .'

A choking gasp drowned her words. Marigold's tears renewed their flow. As though her heart was breaking, she rocked to and fro, let out a loud wail.

Distressed, Tessa ran agitated fingers through her hair.

'All right, then—I'll try, I'll do my best, but I can't say I'm very optimistic.'

Drawing herself up, straightening to her full five foot, five inches, she marched over to the doctor's door, knocked hard upon it. A muffled 'Come in, if you must!' reaching her ears, she swept into the office.

Seated behind a desk stacked high with files and X-ray photographs, Blair Lachlan was dictating into a hand-mike. He was wearing a high-buttoned white jacket and had the well-scrubbed immaculate look of the professional medic. He glanced up, and his brow creased in a deep frown.

'Tessa Maitland—You! I'm not aware that you have an appointment.' His tone was icy.

She drew a breath. 'I haven't, I'm afraid, but I must speak to you—the matter's urgent. Could you—would you—spare me a minute or two?' The words jerked out. 'It's Mari,' she went on, desperately trying to control her nerves. 'She's terribly upset—she said she's to be admitted here immediately, and could have to stay to full term.'

She swallowed. 'Probably you don't know it, but my sister's scared stiff of hospitals.'

The tawny brows shot high. 'She is? Well, how about that? She elected to come here, didn't she, for her confinement? The LS, let me point out, is no ordinary institution; it's a well-established clinic, luxuriously equipped.'

Tessa shuffled her feet. 'Oh, yes, that's very obvious.' Why that wrong emphasis, the note of sarcasm? 'It's just that we—I—wondered . . . well, couldn't Mari be cared for at home equally efficiently? If anything, she should recover more quickly there. Wilma—that's her maid—she can look after the apartment, and I can look after Marigold.'

She cleared her throat. 'You probably don't remember, but I am a trained nurse.'

Amber eyes rounding, he glared across the desk.

'And I'm not exactly senile as yet, my memory still serves me pretty accurately! Your sister, I distinctly recall, made quite a point of mentioning the fact, as if no-one in your family had reached such dizzy heights ever before! Allow me to congratulate you! Forgive me for not doing so earlier!'

A muscle twitched in his lip. 'In view of your extensive and remarkable training, it surprises me that you should question a doctor's orders.'

Anger conquered her nerves.

'And I, Dr Lachlan, am amazed that you gave Mari your decision when she was alone, unaccompanied. Why wasn't I called in to be with her when you broke the news, or Ramon summoned?'

He clapped both hands to his brow. 'For crying out loud! Now, I've heard it all, heard everything! Did I know you were outside? Didn't I suggest bringing Rae over? You maintain that your sister is deeply distressed, yet while in this office she appeared perfectly composed. I offered that my nurse should stay with her, and she calmly refused.'

He scowled. 'You two spark one another off, I guess.'

Her indignation rose. 'Then you guess wrong!' she snapped. 'And I still fail to see why I can't be allowed to nurse my sister in her own home. If she's admitted here and can't settle, it won't do the slightest good.'

Slowly, the doctor unfolded his long limbs, got to his feet. His steps firm, deliberate, he advanced round the desk, lifted one hand high. For one fraught moment, Tessa feared he was about to strike her. Instead, he angrily smote the back of his head, palmed down his hair.

'Listen to me, and listen carefully!' he commanded. 'Let me spell things out, in single syllables, if need be. You agree that it's my duty to give your sister full medical care, do everything in my power to see she's safely delivered of a healthy child? Right!'

He tugged at his jacket collar. 'For weeks, I've been warning Marigold about the danger of getting over-tired, of smoking, of having her blood pressure rise. This afternoon, what do I find? She presents with toxaemia, hypertension, oedema. The tests we carried out confirm that constant observation is advisable, complete bedrest. If her condition should improve after a stay with us, then it is possible I could reconsider my decision. Until that time, she remains where she is, under this roof. Unless she wishes to change her medical adviser, of course . . .'

His wide mouth clamped shut. Tessa's heart sank. The gravity of his tone, the seriousness of his expression, had convinced her that he was right. Mari must stay in the clinic.

Fearful, she glanced towards the door. How to go out there, confront Marigold with the dismal result? If only she could be given a little time to adjust . . . Moistening her lips, she conjured up a smile, gazed up into the stern sunburnt face.

'It'd help, maybe, if you'd allow Mari to drive home, collect what she needs? That way, she'd have a chance to get used to the idea, to advise Rae . . .'

Like a bull about to charge, he lowered his tawny head. Moving forward his eyelids flickered dangerously.

'NO!' he declared, in a near-shout.

She took a step back.

'But . . .' she gulped. Swallowing hard, she searched for a reason that might move him, persuade him to permit her sister a breathing-space. One last throw . . .

'But that big Mercedes Benz, that great car of hers, I can't handle it,' she burst out. 'And even supposing I could, I've never driven on the right, I've only driven in England, and there very little. Mari'll want her negligées, toiletries, personal belongings, and she'll only get more upset if she has to wait. The drive home would give her time to come to terms . . .'

Even as the words tumbled from her trembling lips, she knew them for what they were—an excuse, stupid, contrived. And in the doctor's amber eyes she read his deep contempt, the scorn he felt.

Leaning forward, he gripped her shoulders with iron hands.

'So, you're scared, you can't drive on the right!' Scathingly, his tone mimicked hers. 'Well, Miss Clever Nurse, here's your golden opportunity—now, you can learn, learn to travel the civilised side! And don't you try to wheedle the way Marigold does—you're not very good at it. Your sister's life is in my hands, and that of her unborn child. Do you think I'd let you, or anyone else, influence me in any way at all?'

Tightening, his strong fingers dug into her, pressed into her flesh.

'Get going, Tessa Maitland! Get on your way and stop

wasting my time! I've a round to do, sick people to attend. Get out of my office, and let me do what I'm here to do!'

CHAPTER THREE

THE distance from the LS to 'Los Arboles' was an exact two miles. To Tessa, driving the Mercedes, it seemed more like two hundred. Lacking experience, the very idea filled her with alarm. Only after an attempt to contact Ramon had failed—he was out visiting a supplier—had she thrown all caution to the wind, a flood of tears from Marigold providing the deciding factor.

Even when she'd finally seated herself at the wheel, she'd sat for minutes playing with the controls. Alien, numerous, they had her confused. Could she? Dare she? About to give up, she'd caught a white flicker in her driving mirror. Casting a glance back to the LS, she'd caught the movement of a tall figure at an office window, *his* office window. That second, she'd switched on the ignition, slipped into gear. No way was she letting the LS dictator see her defeated.

Eyes on stalks, ears straining, heart pumping madly, she'd gingerly edged the long body out into the street. The car seemed the size of a bus. What if she crashed it, crumpled those shining wings, dented the diamond bright bodywork, wrote off her sister's prized possession? She quivered with nerves.

At once vehicles swamped her, hooted, shouldered in. The evening rush hour—she'd hit the peak! Which way? Which turn did she take? The route, could she remember it? Perspiration dampened her brow, trickled down her body. The first automobile to pass her on the left sent her into a fit of trembling that lasted a full minute.

Somehow, she made it back. A mass of jangling nerves, she stumbled out, breathed relief as her feet touched ground. Only then as she saw a taxi pull from

51

beneath the portico did she realise there'd been an alternative, an alternative she'd overlooked. Easily, she could have left the Mercedes parked where it was, called a taxi. Agitation had robbed her of reason.

Shakily, she filled the suitcases Wilma whisked out, had her call a hire car. All the way back to the clinic she sat biting her nails. Would Mari come safely through her pregnancy? The precious baby, would it survive? How would Rae take the news about his wife's hospitalisation?

Back at the LS she found Marigold sitting dejectedly in the top floor room she'd been allocated. Small but superbly equipped (Tessa registered a monitor, piped oxygen, a button-operated bed) it had a bathroom and balcony en suite. A sharp-eyed nurse stood taking Marigold's pulse; 'Dagmar Fisher', her name-brooch read.

'You made it safely home? I thought you would.' Marigold smiled wanly. 'Use my car, if you wish. I'll have no need of it in here. And you'll need transport for visiting and marketing. I'll have to ask you to take over running the apartment.'

'That, I'll do gladly,' Tessa agreed. 'But as for driving your car again—not on your Nelly! For the present, I've had the porter tuck it up in the garage. Don't you worry, I'll manage to get around. There are buses, and I have two feet. Here are your things—the immediate essentials; I'll bring the rest in tomorrow.'

Marigold sighed. 'Tomorrow and tomorrow and tomorrow, you'll find me here. Junior's not due for another seventy days, according to my reckoning. And there I was, happily planning all sorts of trips to take you on. It's rotten luck on you, me spoiling your vacation.'

'That's the last thing you should worry about.' Tessa's tone was brisk. 'I'm pleased to be on hand at such a time. The parents, how glad they'll be they sent me over, though for the time being I suggest we don't tell them about this—we don't want them worried unduly.'

She proceeded to unpack while the nurse helped her

new patient to undress and get to bed. A little later Ramon arrived, his face taut with anxiety, and she slipped quietly away. It was best to leave husband and wife together. Planning to wait for her brother-in-law, get him to give her a lift home, she decided to fill in time by taking a walk round the block.

The sun was still lighting the west, but the air had rapidly cooled. Fresh, crisp, it calmed her nerves, but the worry remained; she couldn't think of anything but Mari and her child.

Turning back, she approached the LS. One by one, the lights were going on, yellowing the window panes. How long before Ramon would be ready to leave? Should she ring Wilma and have her keep the supper back?

Mind buzzing, she reached the big entrance, put out a hand to push the plate-glass door. A tall figure shadowed the far side. Too late, she stepped back. Blair Lachlan came stamping out.

'Tessa Maitland! You, still around? Why, in heaven's name . . .'

He came to an abrupt halt, wide lips slanted. 'You don't trust us with your sister, is that it? May I assure you that you can?'

Without the courtesy of a 'Goodnight' he marched towards the parking area. Cheeks flaming, Tessa knew a sudden fierce dislike, one bordering on hate. Why was this sunburnt giant so unfeeling, so unsympathetic? Why rub salt in a raw wound? What had happened to sour the unfathomable doctor? Had that wound scarred his soul?

But for Tony Arretino, Tessa would have found the next few weeks extremely hard going. To the limit, Marigold tried her patience. Constantly, she was on the phone, demanding this or that to be taken in to her, and at once. When it wasn't baby wool, knitting pins, patterns, it was needlepoint, tapestry yarn, embroidery. Books had to be tracked down and purchased, magazines bought by the dozen, sketch pads and pencils procured. The clinic food not being to her liking, Wilma had to be coaxed into preparing special dishes, and these needed transporting. Marigold even insisted on having her personal bed linen. Lying back on soft pillows in a flower filled room, she concentrated on her next demand or complaint. Dagmar Fisher, her special nurse, couldn't put foot, hand, or tongue right. Secretly, Tessa came to suspect her sister was trying to 'work her ticket', get herself discharged.

Even the tolerant Ramon showed signs of strain, of growing irritable with his adored wife. Tessa had to soothe him.

'Expectant mums do require a lot of understanding,' she pointed out. 'Having these unpleasant complications Mari needs more than most.' Tongue in cheek, she spoke.

Tony was her salvation. His gentle voice comforted, his strong arms consoled. But for him, evenings and Sundays would have dragged. Then Marigold had no need of her, for she had Ramon's company. Appointing himself as her guide, Tony escorted Tessa the length and breadth of Santa Fé. They explored from the State Capital complex to the Cross of the Martyrs, from Burro Alley to the Cathedral of St Francis. With him as mentor, Tessa learned much of sculpture, more of painting. No studio was closed to her talented admirer; even after nightfall there were few galleries to which he couldn't gain admittance at a late hour. After they'd eaten a light meal in a modest restaurant, they'd set off to stroll through the lovely city. Hand in hand they went, like contented children.

It was of a child that Tony put Tessa in mind. Like a child, he had a simplicity, a circumscribed outlook. What went on beyond the limit of his vision or experience held no interest, but things close at hand he observed minutely. His roots lay in the New Mexican soil, his inspiration he derived from nature and from the native people. Beyond vouchsafing he was country born, he revealed little of his past. He had mystery; he had glamour.

A few small things about him did occasionally irk Tessa: one was his habitual unpunctuality. Seldom did he manage to turn up at an appointed time. Immersed in his work, he paid scant attention to the passing hours. Often, he'd forget to eat even. And when he did, he was pernickety over food. If not to his liking, he'd push away his plate untouched; seldom did he finish a full helping. But Tessa had to admit that American servings did tend to be over-generous and waste of food a national trait. The land running with milk and buffalo had bred prodigality.

Tony utterly despised automobiles. The world, he claimed, was being rapidly ruined by the internal combustion engine. Soon, it would be obliged to revert to horse and ox power. Contemplating this simpler form of existence, he'd speak with the conviction of a prophet, and his eyes would hold the shine of a visionary. In him Tessa saw a man of total honesty, of whole-hearted dedication. Ramon's faith in his protégé would be repaid one hundredfold, she felt certain.

Revelling in Tony's company, she didn't feel she was missing out on her holiday, though her eyes would often lift to the distant hills and she'd long to go further afield.

Gradually Marigold's friends took on much of the clinic visiting, organised a roster. To Tessa this was a two-fold blessing. In addition to saving time and energy, it reduced the risk of running into Dr Lachlan.

From the day of their clash, she'd taken considerable care to avoid him, noting when it was he made his rounds, the hours he arrived and departed. On every occasion she entered the LS she cast a cautious eye towards the parking lot, checked to see if his red Porsche stood in the reserved rectangle. All approaches to the medical staff she left to Ramon. Marigold, she knew, continued to pester to be allowed home but the doctor remained adamant that she needed to be an in-patient.

With more time at her disposal, Tessa fulfilled her promise to visit Rosita Ruiz. Several times Conchita had repeated the invitation when they'd happened to meet in Marigold's room.

The invalid was delighted to see her. Once begun, the calls became an almost daily occurrence. Despite her physical limitations, Rosita displayed a lively interest in the world beyond her windows and could converse on a wide variety of topics. Tessa found her a rewarding companion. Anxious to learn more about her past, she was watchful for a suitable opening. One presented itself when Rosita complained about her legs, one morning.

'Look how flabby they've become!' Morosely, she pointed down.

Tessa shrugged. 'That's hardly surprising, seeing that they're not exercised. Physiotherapy might be an idea—it could help restore muscle tone.'

Rosita fluttered a dismissive hand. 'I've tried it. For weeks, a physio called in regularly. Then she moved away and we didn't bother any more. What does it matter? The treatment did no good.'

'Maybe it didn't continue long enough? I'm no expert, but I have seen some remarkable results. Why not ask Dr Sepulveda his opinion, find out if he considers another course worth while?'

She sought an inducement. 'When Mari's baby comes, she'll be wanting help with it. And when it starts to run about, you'll be wanting to join in the play, and the games.'

Rosita pursed her lips, looked down at her hands. 'There was a time when I dreamt of playing with children of my own. I had something good going with a fine man . . . Now, I don't care to think of the future, but live only for the day. Tell me about your sister; how sick is she, actually? Mama and I feel very concerned.'

The change of tack wasn't lost on Tessa but she had to let it ride. A curtain had dropped between Rosita and herself; once again, she had to wait. But what she had learned served to strengthen her suspicion that more lay behind Rosita's tragedy than had been revealed. She had had a romance; there'd been a man friend, one whom she'd loved and lost. When? How? Why?

She felt a great urge to discover more. Who would know the background? Conchita, could she approach her?

One of Marigold's main tribulations was that Tessa wasn't getting in on the local scene, wasn't socialising sufficiently.

'If I weren't condemned to lie here like a stranded whale, you'd be out and around and meeting folk.' She slapped her middle. 'Hi, you in there! Junior, it's all your fault! Oh, well, never mind—rescue will soon be on hand. Very soon, the Emerys will be back from their vacation in Europe—they're our closest SF buddies. Anna's Swiss, Vance is Californian, and you'll adore them. They'll introduce you around. And just wait till you see their home—it's fabulous! They're loaded. Vance made a pile out of real estate.'

What, Tessa wondered idly, was *un*real estate? American certainly took a little learning.

In the ensuing days, Marigold made frequent reference to Anna Emery. Her elegance was lauded, her kindness, her charm, her prowess as a hostess. Hearing her praises sung so high and so often, Tessa was almost afraid to meet the paragon for fear of being disappointed. But one morning there she was, seated by Marigold's bed. Big, blonde, blue-eyed and beautiful, soigné in black linen with white accessories, she looked all that had been claimed. She was preparing to depart as Tessa went into the room.

'Ah, here is my noble sister!' Marigold exclaimed. 'You two, I've been longing to have you meet—Anna, this is Tessa; Mrs Emery, Miss Maitland. Anna and Vance got in only very late last night, yet here she is to see me, already. Sit down, the pair of you, get acquainted.'

'I've stayed long enough,' Anna protested. 'You mustn't get overtired.' Her low voice held a gutteral undertone. 'Good to know you, Tessa. Now we're back,

you must come and visit often—I'll be giving you a call,
will fix for you to meet some special folk.' She winked at
Marigold. 'Be seeing you!'

'How's that for chic?' Marigold asked, as the door
clicked shut. 'That suit had "Dior" written all over it,
and those accessories were "Gucci", that's for sure.'

'I liked her, she has kind eyes,' Tessa said. 'That
invitation, I'll look forward to it.'

She hadn't long to wait. On Friday evening, the telephone rang.

'Anna here—Emery, remember? You . . . well?
Would you . . . free tomor . . . night?' The line crackled
loudly and the sound came and went. 'You could be?
. . . excellent! We'd love . . . have you . . . our guest at
the Festival dinner-dance; it's a . . . dress occasion.
Sorry . . . short advice . . . a long standing fixture but a
guest just cancel . . .' The line had a fit of atmospherics.
'Around eight . . . send . . . car to bring you . . . restaurant. We'll drive you back . . . wiedersehen.'

Emotions mixed, Tessa replaced the receiver, her
excitement was tinged with guilt as her acceptance
would mean letting Tony down on their regular Saturday
date. But with the chance to wine, dine, dance, meet
people, she'd not been able to resist accepting. And it
would give her an opportunity, the first one she'd had, to
wear her one formal gown, a couturier model she'd won
in a 'Friends of the Hospital' raffle.

In one way the invitation had come at a most opportune time. At weekends, Marigold had a full visiting
list, and there was no need for her to spend time at the
clinic. Instead, she could find a good hairdresser, get a
proper manicure. At all costs she must be a credit to
Mari and Rae, keep up with their jet-set friends.

Eight o'clock the next evening found her seated in the
back of a chauffeur-driven white Cadillac. Her dress of
midnight blue brocade had a daring cleavage, long
sleeves, floating over-panels of chiffon to the skirt.
Round her neck she wore a mass of looped gilt chains,
over her shoulders a black lacy shawl. The beautician

who'd fixed her hair had talked her into a professional maquillage, had liberally applied expensive cosmetics. Lavishly sprayed with French perfume borrowed from Mari, she felt a million dollars.

The limousine delivered her to a five-star restaurant. The uniformed doorman stared hard as he let her in, and so did the major-domo. Tessa preened herself, assured that she looked the part. 'The Emery Party,' she murmured.

A waiter conducted her through to the dining-room. A blast of music hit her ears, a cascade of conversation. Two other things immediately impinged: the lighting came from candles stuck into tallow-coated wine bottles, not from the crystal chandeliers, and the tables were covered in red gingham, not stiff white damask. But the biggest shock was the attire of the diners. Instead of men in tuxedos and women in evening gowns, she beheld cowboys and Indians, ladies in bustles and crinolines, girls dressed like Annie of 'Get your Gun' fame.

Her blood running chill, she caught the waiter's elbow.

'There m-must be some m-mistake,' she stuttered. 'You have another dining-room, maybe, another function on? It's the Emerys, I'm joining.'

The waiter grinned. 'Look straight ahead, Ma'am, and you'll see them. This is tonight's special function—the Festival "Wild West" gala. Too bad you didn't get to know, Ma'am; you'd look great as a cowgirl!'

Her legs like lead, she stood rooted to the floor; never had she felt so utterly foolish, so completely out of place. The door, she must get to the door. She swung on her heel.

A hand fell on her shoulder, a soft southern voice spoke in her ear. Half-turning, she saw a mustachio'd Confederate soldier.

He smiled down. 'Tessa? I'm Vance—Vance Emery; Anna sent me to lead you over. Good to meet you, Tessa. That band, I can hardly hear myself speak—let's head for our corner.'

Still the urge to flee remained; she had to force her feet to follow him. If only the ground would open, swallow her up!

Anna rushed to greet her, an uncertain smile on her face.

'Oh, Tessa, what a pity! That dreadful line, my silly accent! You didn't catch the costume bit? Mari, she has outfits . . . Never mind, it doesn't matter, not in the least. There'll be others . . .'

Taking her hand, she led her firmly to the table, introduced the other guests. Momentarily, Tessa disliked every costumed one. Their voices were too hearty, their smiles too broad in reassurance. Miserably, she flopped into the chair Vance pulled out at the far end of the table, accepted the glass of wine that he poured.

He nodded towards the facing vacant place.

'Any minute your partner'll be here,' he said. 'Something must've kept him.'

She looked down at her dress. This man, when he did arrive, how would he react when he saw her? What would he think of her over-formal attire? She felt sick with misery, with disappointment. Shivering, she blamed herself for not checking out the invitation, for letting Tony down on their date. This was a just retribution for her desertion; she longed to be with him in some quiet spot. Dejectedly, she rustled through her evening bag, sought a tissue.

The empty chair scraped back. Slowly, she lifted her gaze. Taking in dark slacks, a cream tuxedo, her heart leapt. Fortune was smiling—her partner was wearing conventional clothes!

On and up her eyes travelled over a tall figure, reached lean cheeks, and she gaped. The eyes she found herself looking into were clear amber: Blair Lachlan stood staring down.

Mute, they stared at one another. Vividly, too vividly, Tessa recalled their last meeting, remembered the anger, the acrimony. And here she was, doomed to spend an entire evening with the domineering doctor!

Her stomach turned over.

He, it was, who first found voice. 'Good evening, Tessa Maitland.' His drawl lacked its usual vigour. Sinking on to a chair, he flicked out a white handkerchief, mopped his brow. 'Is my face red!' he muttered. 'Come Monday, a certain lady'll get to hear my views about incomplete entries in my engagement book!'

She knew a fleeting elation. Debra Petersen, it just had to be her!

'I can only blame an indistinct phone line,' she commented. 'At least, there are now two of us . . .'

'How come that makes things any better?' he demanded. 'What fools we'll look later, dancing country and western.'

'Dancing WHAT?' Her voice rose shrill. 'Oh no, I couldn't . . .' Hands trembling, she fingered the stiff brocade. A fine sight she'd look, gallumphing up and down with all the Clint Eastwoods and John Waynes! 'This isn't for me,' she went on. 'The minute dinner's over and people move from the table, I'm getting out of here.'

'Oh, no, you're not!' he snapped. 'Anna's planned her numbers exact for the sets—I've counted round the table. There's got to be another way . . . For mercy's sake, wipe that funereal look off your face—this isn't a matter of life and death! Trust me, I'll figure something. Relax—here comes our chow.'

She ate, but didn't taste, the baked clams, the honey-basted duck, the strawberries in Kirsch. Trepidation defeated her taste-buds and with every passing minute it increased.

'Got it!' The exclamation made her start; the doctor leant forward. 'With luck, this can be fixed while the coffee-drinking goes on. We're leaving right now. You head for the foyer while I snatch a word with Vance.'

He came bounding out, a towering figure in a frantic hurry. Grasping her hand, he pulled her into the street.

'Quick march, first turn left,' he ordered.

'But where—what . . . ?' she gasped, running to try to

keep up with him. Those great long legs, what steps they took! Stumbling, she almost fell; he tightened his grip.

'Your nails are digging in!' she cried. 'My skirt's tripping me . . .'

'Then lift it, woman, and stop bleating!' Over his shoulder, he tossed the words. At that moment she saw him as an Army man, tough, ruthless, determined. A shiver of fear went through her. Where was he taking her?

The answer was soon revealed. Pounding to a halt outside a photographic salon, he pointed to a sign in the window:

'VISITORS! TAKE HOME A NEW MEXICAN MEMENTO!—HAVE YOUR PICTURE TAKEN IN PIONEER GEAR! COSTUME SUPPLIED.'

He banged on the door.

'Hal, the guy who owns this place, is a long-time patient, he'll fit us out,' he said.

It was one of those near-instant transformations, the sort sometimes seen on stage. A 1980s Dr Lachlan and Miss Maitland went in. An 1880s US officer and his lady came out.

The photographer fell over himself to assist.

'Little enough to do for you, Doc, after what you've done for me,' he said. Costumes provided, he undertook to pack up, and deliver back, their own attire.

Blair Lachlan paused on the pavement, awarded Tessa a glance of approval, flicked his eyes over her blue cotton gown.

'That's my girl!' he said. 'That Fifth Avenue glitter, that call girl gloss, I didn't care for. Here, take my arm.'

Thrilling at the warm note in his voice, Tessa was glad that she'd tissued off the heavy make-up, had tumbled out the lacquered curls.

There wasn't a dull moment, right from the time they arrived back in the restaurant. The diners had drifted out on to a lantern-lit patio, an MC disguised as a sheriff was arranging the opening dance. From a dais beneath the colonnade the band struck up.

Merrily, the gaily clad couples skipped and tripped, circled to the lively tunes, clapped their hands, swung round. The air shivered with noise and excitement. Warmed by the exertion, people threw off stetsons and bonnets, jackets and shawls, loosened cravats, unfastened collars. Clutched close to Blair, Tessa could feel the warmth of his body through his unbuttoned shirt, the springiness of the tawny curls matting his powerful chest. Strong shoulders weaving, slim hips swinging, he towered above the other men. A born leader, it was he who sorted out tangles when they arose, who kept their set on the move. Filled with pride that she was his partner, Tessa found herself marvelling that she'd ever disliked the man. Off duty he was a different person, relaxed, dishy, dynamic.

All too soon the party was ending. The lights dimmed, the 'Goodnight Waltz' started up. Held tight by his arms she was more than ever aware of the hardness of his body, the thud of his heart. This, if only it could go on and on . . . never stop . . .

The final note faded. Opening her eyes, she met his quizzical stare.

'You've come back?' he asked softly. 'You looked as you did that first night—in another world. Then, I suspected you'd been "sent" by Arretino—a most alarming thought.'

The full lips slanted in a smile. 'Now, I see the reaction's more general. What is it, that puts you in a trance?'

She spread her hands. 'Dreamy music, a partner in step . . .'

The smile widened. 'So, in one respect I'm able to match our budding artist! In what others, I wonder . . . ?'

With one swift jerk he tugged her behind a vine-draped pillar, crushed her to him.

'Tell me,' he demanded, 'My lips, do they come up to

his?' His mouth descended on hers, framed it in a long bruising kiss. The blood coursed through her veins; she shivered a long shiver of desire. The taste, the touch . . .

'Tessa! Tes—sa! Where are you?' Anna Emery's gutteral voice cut the air. 'We're on our way!'

A muttered curse, a harsh intake of breath, and he released her, shook clenched fists. 'Of all times to choose . . . !'

Swallowing hard, Tessa smoothed down her dress, stepped out into the patio.

'Ah! Didn't I say we'd find you here?' Anna waved from the gate leading to the street. 'The car's this side. You had a good time?'

Profoundly, at that moment, Tessa regretted her hostess's efficiency. All she could do was to nod.

The Cadillac's big engine purred smoothly, the wheels sped over the ground. Her heart still racing, Tessa leant her head against the black velvet cushions, shut her eyes, rested her hands in her lap. She just couldn't believe what had happened.

The touch of her skirt against her fingers set her lips twitching. Fine brocade, she'd started out in; in simple cotton, she was going back—this was 'Cinderella' in reverse! The plainer gown, she greatly preferred; it was more 'her'. Blair had liked it; he'd called her his girl. Why was it he hadn't married?

Able to wave a wand, she'd have made one change, substituted a red Porsche for the white Cadillac. A perfect ending . . .

Drowsily, she took in the Emerys' low-voiced dialogue. One party over, they were planning their next. Who would they be asking?

CHAPTER FOUR

'Come on, give! I'm dying to hear all about the gala dance!'

Marigold was avid for details. 'Anna and Vance dropped by earlier. According to them, you and Blair made their party. Clever of him, wasn't it, to hunt up those costumes? Nothing defeats our Dr L.'

The violet eyes twinkled. 'Told you, didn't I, that he's not some kind of ogre! Vance's highly chuffed that he had such a splendid time, said it's ages since he's seen him let his hair down.'

'He knows Blair well?'

'Since High School, on and off. They met up again when Blair got back from Vietnam, covered in glory.'

She flicked Tessa a mischievous glance.

'Guess who it was you replaced at the party? Green eyes herself! Last minute Friday La Petersen cancelled, not entirely to the Emerys' displeasure. They're not overkeen on the lady and don't consider her suitable for Blair. It was him who elected to take her along.'

Tessa narrowed her gaze. 'How come she didn't make the date?'

'Patience, little sister, and all will be revealed.' Marigold lifted a hand. 'From what "Fish" told me— hey, hike me up a bit, will you? This darned bed, I keep slipping down.'

Arranging the pillows armchair style, Tessa had to smile. So it was 'Fish' now was it? Dagmar Fisher having become a reliable source of hospital gossip, Marigold had developed a liking for the nurse. This time, what had she discovered?

'Thanks a lot.' Marigold nestled back. 'Where was I? Oh, yes. "Fish" said that her pal in Reception told her she caught high words being passed between DP and BL at the end of the week and heard dear Debra pull out of the date. And that's not all—earlier today there was another slanging match followed by a making-up. Now the two are friends again. The path of true love, it never runs smooth.'

Tessa's heart sank, and Marigold's next words did nothing to lift it.

'If I were you, I'd watch out, be wary of that dame. She's one hundred per cent cat, I gather. The kind to scratch and claw, at any trespassing on her property. It's a crying shame she's stuck her paws into Blair.'

Tessa had been walking on air; like a lead balloon she descended to earth and felt as if she'd landed in an icy pool. The Blair-Petersen relationship wasn't confined to doctor-secretary roles. That first evening, there'd been an inkling . . . The ash-blonde was beautiful, very beautiful, but those eyes were terribly cold. Could it be that they looked different when turned on the opposite sex, looked warm?

She kept a wary eye open on leaving the LS. No longer fearful that she might run into Blair, she'd gone happily swinging in, hoping that he might be around. Now, spirits dampened, she made a cautious exit. Needing to cheer herself up, she went to see Rosita.

She, too, was eager to hear about the festival ball, having heard of Tessa's invitation from Conchita who'd had the news from Rae who'd been informed by Vance . . . Santa Fé was certainly a closely knit community.

Listening to the details, Rosita widened her eyes.

'A fly on the wall, that's what I'd like to have been!' she said. 'Country and Western was something I used to adore, one time.' Her face saddened. 'But there, it wouldn't have been that much fun, just looking on. I'd have only grown miserable, knowing I'll never dance again.'

'Never give up!' Reproachfully, Tessa shook her head. 'How do you know? There's always hope . . .'

Rosita grimaced. 'Exactly Sep's words, when he last

called in. By the way, he is finding me another physio—thinks therapy could be worth another whirl. Once more, he got on his favourite hobby horse, went on about my getting out, said I ought to see the trees in their fall colours.'

'Then why don't you? Couldn't we find someone with a car that could accommodate your chair?' Tessa was immediately enthusiastic.

'No, no, not yet!' Panic edging her voice, Rosita shrank back. 'Thank you, but really, I'd rather not. It's been a while since I went outside this apartment. Here, I've learnt to be content, to cope with my limitations which are infinitely more inhibiting outside. And the rush, the bustle, the noise, even in little Santa Fé, can be frightening after being indoors.'

She made a wide sweep of her hand. 'I've everything I need here, within these four walls. Friends drop by, a beautician calls to do my hair, a dressmaker comes in. This way, I avoid getting dissatisfied.'

Her gaze travelled beyond the balcony, down to the spacious lawns. 'Very occasionally, I do get a great longing, a desire for change. Strangely, it's the simple things I miss most of all, the joy of walking on grass, strolling along a pebbly shore, climbing a river bank . . .'

Tessa's throat tightened. She could indulge in these little pleasures any time she wished, without a thought.

'Above all else, I crave to be independent,' Rosita went on, and sighed. 'But there it is. Not being able to walk . . .'

Tessa turned her head, to hide her misted eyes. Independence, too, she took for granted. Surreptitiously, she brushed away a tear. Rosita was in a talkative mood; she must concentrate. This could be a chance to find out about her past.

'This—paralysis, it came on suddenly?' she ventured.

Rosita bit her lip. 'No—it kind of crept up on me. First, my legs grew weak, tired quickly. It became difficult to stand. Eventually, I couldn't walk.'

She hunched her shoulders. 'It was a ghastly time.

First, papa was taken from us, then we lost our old home. The estancia had been in the family for generations. Until the last will and testament was read, we'd no idea about the heavy debts, the huge mortgage. Our lovely house had to go, the horses . . .'

Her voice sank. 'Before that, even, things had started to go wrong. The—friend I mentioned, I'd had to send him away, tell him a lie. My conscience, it never rests.' Against her breast, she made the sign of the cross. 'I'm not boring you?'

Tessa edged her chair closer. 'Not a bit—I'm very interested. I'm a nurse, don't forget, and nurses need to be good listeners. You were saying . . . ?'

Rosita gave a wan smile of gratitude. 'You're very simpatico. It's such a relief, being able to talk. For hours on end I sit here, in Buddha-like contemplation. Mama's a darling, but she has a lot on her hands, is always in a hurry. Anyway, I'd not want to stir up painful memories for her. So no-one has time to be an ear, and I get lost in nostalgia, sunk in the past. Constantly, my mind goes back to happier days.'

For a while she stayed silent, sat fingering the gold crucifix at her neck as though summoning strength. When she spoke again, her voice was little more than a whisper.

'My friend wasn't New Mexican, or from our kind of family. In many ways, we didn't match up—religion, education, social standing—whatever that may mean— but at heart we were one. The differences didn't concern me one little bit—I never gave them a thought—but they did worry my parents, papa particularly. The Ruiz, you see, had married into property for centuries, usually into the families of adjacent landowners, and papa was ambitious for me.'

'The top brick off the chimney, that's what fathers commonly want for their daughters,' Tessa murmured.

Rosita nodded. 'That's exactly how it was. At first, I was deaf to all protestations, but then when he got sick his grief seemed to aggravate his illness. Loving him as I did, I couldn't proceed against his wishes. In our sort of family, blood is a great tie.'

She bowed her head. 'Now, it's hard to believe, but then my future was bright with promise, the promise that every woman longs to have—love, marriage, a family. At a blow, all was finished, and I was the one who had to deal that blow.'

She sighed heavily. 'To try to help my father, I decided I must end my romance, and there had to be an excuse. So I told my lover a falsehood, made pretend there was someone else. The story did hold a germ of truth—my parents had been hopeful that I'd marry the wealthy heir to a nearby estancia but later on, when I found out about the debts, I felt even more guilty that I'd rejected him. The money could've helped them . . .'

She paused. 'To this day, I long for my lover, wonder where he is, if he married . . .'

'What was he like? What did he do? Where was he from?' Eagerly, the questions burst from Tessa's lips. Too late, she realised they'd been over quick, had smacked of intrusion; too late, she observed the deep frown.

Rosita slumped in her wheel-chair. 'Another time, maybe. I feel too tired.'

Tessa's mind was spinning when she left her friend. The story she'd just heard had confirmed her suspicion, the suspicion that Rosita's past had held a secret. The loss of a loved father, that had been severe, but the loss of a lover surely a more likely reason for her giving up on life? A contributory cause to her disability? The mind possessed immense power over the body; over and over again, she'd seen proof in her work on the wards.

Her heart ached for her friend. Setback on setback, sacrifice upon sacrifice, disaster after disaster. Suffering such a train of sorrow, was it any wonder that Rosita had withdrawn from the world, hidden herself away?

How best could she help? One thing she'd just learned was that it wouldn't be advisable to consult Conchita. But how else could she get any clue as to the identity of the vanished suitor? Discover his whereabouts? A re-union, that was what was needed. To bring the pair together again—but was it possible? Her thoughts in a turmoil, she went to keep her postponed date with Tony.

He was waiting by the obelisk in the plaza, their usual meeting place. Even in his faded denims he managed to look exotic, and his sturdy figure exuded reassurance.

'Long time, no see!' He held out his arms.

'What, two days a long time?' she chided, savouring his ardent embrace.

They strolled beneath the trees, and he grudgingly asked if she'd enjoyed the festival evening. Seeking to amuse him, she described the initial débâcle, the foray for costumes. To her chagrin, she saw his face darken.

'So, our medicine man tried to muscle in, did he? That, I can't allow, not even if he is my medic, and the best around! No way is he going to pinch my girl.' He squeezed her arm.

'But he didn't . . .' she began, only to be cut short.

'No, and I'll see to it that he doesn't! He was welcome to the cavorting—it's not my line—but your company, that's something else.' Hungrily, his eyes feasted on hers. 'Today, where've you been? Where've you spent your time?' His tone held suspicion.

'First, to see Mari, then to call on Ramon's sister,' she replied. A sudden impulse made her add: 'Rosita, do you know her? Have you met her?'

'Yep, I have made her acquaintance. Took some paintings over to the apartment for her to view one time, when Rae wanted to make her a gift. Very pretty, I thought she was. Why do you ask?'

'I want to find out all I can about her, about what happened.'

'Then I'm not your man. I got to know Ramon only after he opened up the gallery, two years or so back. The one occasion we did get to meet, I got the impression of someone somewhat uptight, like she had a secret sor-row. And strong-willed, yes, I remember thinking she was strong-willed: she wasn't going to accept a picture she didn't like.'

Tessa gazed in admiration. Those gipsy eyes, how much they saw, how little they missed. Urgently, she needed a confidant, and Tony was the soul of discretion. How to start?

'What are you up to, Tessa?' Before she could open her mouth, he'd read her thoughts. The floodgates opened, and she poured out her theory, her ideas concerning Rosita, her desire to trace the vanished lover.

'Hm-mmm.' Long drawn, the murmur conveyed doubt. 'Should you interfere, try to play match-maker? The guy could be married, by now. And if he's not and you manage to find him the chemistry mightn't work, after three years. I'd say you're taking on too great a load.'

'But it's worth a try, surely? Remember what's at stake—Rosita's future. Imagine, she might even get to walk again!'

'And she might not. How do you know this is what she actually wants? Take care, Tess; reaching for the stars, you could fall on your face. But enough of that—there's something more pressing to discuss. It's high time we got started on your portrait.'

Next afternoon he began, and it took a while for him to make the necessary preparation. Tessa arrived at the studio to find him tossing a stack of odds and ends from the model's throne, and then it had to be dusted. Finally established on the high-backed chair, she was directed to turn this way and that, to try out various poses. A decision arrived at, Tony embarked on a preliminary sketch.

'Ramon's still not too happy about my doing your picture,' he confided, scratching crayon on paper. 'His one preoccupation is to have me conveyor-belt animal and cowhand studies for stock; there'll come a time when I'll throw up, at the sight of a bison! The day I dream about is when I can paint what I want, when I wish; when I won't be beholden.'

He glanced towards her. 'Talk as much as you like, provided you don't shift that pose. Half-time, we'll take a break.'

The session over, he bade her wait while he chalked her outline on throne and dais. While he did so her gaze wandered round the cluttered studio. How ever could anyone exist, let alone manage to work, in such an appalling muddle? Her fingers itched to clean and tidy.

'Be sure to wear that same dress, every sitting,' he requested. 'That sapphire blue enhances the colour of your lovely eyes.'

Tenderly, he lifted her from the little platform, held her close. At once, she forgot the confusion and disarray, the pungent smell of turpentine and paint. Only the comforting nearness of him she knew, the smoothness of his olive skin, the robustness of his body.

'I don't need to tell you I've taken a tumble, fallen in love?' He sought her lips, kissed her hard and long. When he found voice, it was with a jerk of his dark head towards the hardboard partition.

'Evenings, you could visit here,' he suggested. 'My pad, it's not classy, but we'd be comfortable.'

Tessa knew a quickening of her pulse, but she shook her head. Night-time, the gallery was closed, there was no-one around. Alone in the studio with him, there'd be temptation . . .

'Rae might get to hear,' she pointed out. 'He could disapprove, and we're both in his debt. We don't want to upset him, and that could be a risk.'

But it was a danger of a very different kind she had in mind, as she spoke.

It didn't take Ramon long to reveal his concern regarding the way Tony was employing his time.

'I don't want to seem dog-in-manger,' he told Tessa, 'but I'd greatly appreciate your co-operation. Try to see Tony doesn't go overboard on your picture. He could get carried away, neglect work that's been commissioned. Our pre-Christmas exhibition's not that far off, and I need every study he can turn out—it's essential that he keeps his nose to the grindstone. Both of us can use the cash, and he has his reputation to build.'

They were sharing one of their rare at-home suppers. Since Marigold's admittance to the LS, Ramon seldom found time to return to 'Los Arboles' until late evening. For him, meals had shortened to snacks snatched between gallery and clinic.

'Right now, life's kind of costly,' he confided. 'What with increasing inflation, the high interest I've to meet on the loan I took to open the gift shop, I have a lot on my plate. Of course, when I planned that extension I hadn't an inkling that Mari'd not be fit for months on end. Over here, hospitalisation comes costly; insurance covers around eighty per cent, only. Well-to-do folk, even, can get bankrupted when they hit a long spell of sickness.'

He tugged at his beard. 'In the end, all that matters is that Mari makes it safely through this pregnancy and we have a healthy kid, but the cash must be kept rolling. Tony's a gifted artist, but like most of his kind, he lacks a head for business. And he's not that reliable.'

Defensive words sprang to Tessa's lips, but one quick look at Ramon made her bite them back. His face was grey with anxiety, and the hazel eyes had lost their twinkle. In place of the 'Laughing Cavalier' she saw a worried husband.

'In addition, there's Rosita's expenses to cover,' he was saying. 'If only she could get better, do something with her life. It's not just the money, I want her to be happy, lead a meaningful existence. There've been times, I have to admit, when I've wondered if she really wants to recover, but I know it's uncharitable to entertain such a thought.'

'Something to live for, to spur her on, that's what she needs,' Tessa said. 'The other day, she mentioned a romance she had, before your father died. Did you ever get to meet the man?'

Ramon clicked his tongue. 'No, though I did hear

tell . . . As I think I mentioned, I was over in Europe around that period.'

Thoughtfully, he twirled the ends of his moustache. 'What I do recall is that the parents didn't approve, they wrote me about that; they didn't consider Rosita's beau good enough. A bit of snobbery could've come into it, they tended to resist change. Mama, bless her, has caught up with the times since then, fortunately.'

Very fortunately, Tessa thought; otherwise, Marigold wouldn't have stood a chance. Earlier, she'd not have made the grade, being only a shopkeeper's daughter. Now, there was a Ruiz glad to be in the retail trade.

She switched her mind back to her question.

'You don't remember any details about the boyfriend? His name, what work he did?'

Ramon's eyes narrowed. 'His job—yes, that fact did lodge in my mind. He was some sort of government employee, a boffin on top-level work. I recall the parents complaining they could find no common ground, their world being one of land and stock, his one of science. But now, I must get my skates on.'

Rising, he gave his customary bow.

'Mari'll be giving me up, else; earlier on, she had a gaggle of visitors going in, so I thought I'd wait a little. Goodnight, Tessa—don't forget what I said. Keep Tony hard at work!'

His last words were lost on her. Open-mouthed, she stared after him. At last, she had a line! The missing Romeo, he was a scientist, a civil servant or the American equivalent. That kind of professional shouldn't be too hard to find. His name—all she wanted now was his name!

Absent-mindedly, her thoughts still on how to further the search, she strolled into the LS next morning. Going from bright sunlight into cool shade, her eyes didn't focus immediately, and she didn't take in the tall figure. Only when the doctor skidded to a halt on the glassy tiles did she stop with a start. Her heart gave a little leap.

'Hi, there!' He flourished an arm. 'Good to see you, Tessa Maitland! Four days, it's been. You still do have feet, after our rustic hop? It sure was fun. One evening soon, we must hunt out another C & W, and go ready kitted! It's been a long while since I had myself such a ball!'

The door leading to his office had slid quietly open, a neat figure stood listening.

'Marigold's doing well,' Blair Lachlan went on. 'A few minutes back, I looked in on her. Her bp's coming down, she reports fewer head pains . . .'

Debra Petersen's voice rang out across the vestibule.

'Dr Lachlan, I've something that's urgent . . .'

He went racing off. 'See you!' he called back.

The green eyes met Tessa, signalled a message.

'In hell first,' they read.

'Taos, how about our taking a trip to Taos, this weekend?' Tony suggested, the next time Tessa saw him. 'The Indian pueblo there is coming up for six centuries old—it's one of the New Mexican wonders. And the town's a thriving art centre. I've good friends there who'd accommodate us Saturday night.'

'Taos! That'd be super! It's one of the 'musts' on my list,' Tessa said excitedly. 'But a whole weekend—I'd not want to be away that long; Mari might need me. Couldn't we make it there and back, in just the one day?'

Staying the night away, that was better avoided. Her father's advice rang in her ears: 'Before you share lodgings with a man, be sure to get a ring on your finger!'

Tony shrugged. 'Could do, if you insist; it's only seventy miles. I thought you'd like a longer break.'

Inwardly, Tessa was amused. How many times had she recently hinted that she'd like to take a trip into the hills, hints that he'd chosen to ignore because he hated to travel? This sudden consideration, could it have anything to do with a certain doctor, with the festival dance?

Taos! She thrilled at the thought. Before coming to New Mexico, she'd heard tell of the ancient town hidden in the Sangre de Cristo mountains, heard how the early trading post had become a place of pilgrimage for writers and artists from all over the world, D. H. Lawrence among their number. And to get up into the high plateaux, the towering peaks, had been her ambition since she'd set foot in the State. Every morning, every evening, she'd lifted her eyes to the shining summits.

For once, Tony managed not to be late. Right on time for the bus, he was waiting at the stop, a darkly exotic figure dressed in denim. The single decker they boarded had a glass top and wide windows. They took the front seat.

'It's a modern crystal coach!' Tessa exclaimed. His gipsy eyes smiling into hers, Tony took her hand in his, and she knew a glow of happiness.

Northward they sped, along Highway 68, crossed wide valleys. Up, up, up, the road steadily climbed, thrusting between stately poplars, ribbed orchards, farm land. Outside the scattered adobe cottages they passed thick ropes of chillis hung from porch posts and there were strings of variegated Indian corn, pink inter-mingled with purple, blue with green, the rich harvest of summer put out to dry against the lean days of winter.

The higher they went into the hills, the greater Tessa's excitement grew. The scenery seemed all too vivid to be true; sharply etched, the mountains stood out against the blue sky like a magnificent stage-drop. As the bus drove into Taos she was obliged to blink her eyes, pinch her arm, to make sure it was all real. Above towered the sacred peak, purple-robed, around spread narrow wind-ing streets. Her ears popped with the altitude, her eyes brightened with admiration.

The moment they set foot in the ancient plaza, she was transported back in time. The quaint two-storeyed buildings she saw not as smart boutiques, art galleries, restaurants, but in their original guise of homes, stables, smithies. In place of the rows of gleaming automobiles she imagined heavy wagons, frisky horses, Wells Fargo coaches. To this town had ridden war-like Apaches, traders from the Santa Fé trail, Kit Carson, the renowned Indian agent. The primitive pueblo was a revelation.

'Do high-rise flats really date back six hundred years?' Tessa asked, gazing astonished at the adobe apartment blocks. In stepped tiers, the terracotta buildings rose from the terracotta earth, as if grown from the soil.

Originally, the homes at ground level had had no doors, access being gained through holes in the roofs reached by removable ladders. That way, there was protection from marauders.

The few faces peering at them from the windows were all wizened. With a rule that all inhabitants must be safely indoors before nightfall, the village had become a dwelling place of the old, rather than the young.

Finding a tree-shaded spot by a stream, they ate the picnic Wilma had packed for them. The air was cooler than in Santa Fé, and held a tangy freshness. The willow-patterned sky seemed to reach right to the ground, and the brilliant light was dazzling.

'The Indians believe it has the power to bring well-being to the soul,' Tony said, and she noticed that his voice was lower than usual. Inexplicably, they found themselves conversing in hushed tones all the time, so strange was the effect of sky and light. It gave Tessa a feeling of buoyancy, of weightlessness.

It was while they were eating their frankfurters that Tony revealed he had a call to make, on Ramon's behalf. Hearing of their destination he'd requested that Tony should call on an out-worker he employed to settle an account. A weaver by the name of Inez, a mutual acquaintance, she was distrustful of banks and preferred payment in cash.

The town explored, they made their way to the outskirts and sought out the weaver's hogan. Roly-poly plump, dark-eyed, sallow-skinned, Inez welcomed them in. Dressed in a home-spun fawn shift, her greying hair liberally sprinkled with fluff from the wool she'd been spinning, she had a soft fuzzy look; Tessa was put in mind of a life-size teddy bear, a human Mrs Bruin. In a matter of minutes she had her guests seated out in a tiny patio, cool drinks in their hands, a dish of tortillas before them.

For a while, the conversation was desultory, general. When her companions went on to discuss the local art and craft scene, Tessa sat back to listen. Sipping her glass of fresh lime, she remarked a certain similarity between the weaver and the painter, both in features and in colouring. Could they be related?

Certainly, they were close friends. Inez made no secret of her affection for Tony. Whenever she passed him food, went to refill his glass, her hand lingered on his; all the time, she sat with her eyes fixed upon him. To Tessa the devotion was irritating to watch, almost embarrassing, and she leapt up with alacrity when a visit to the workroom was suggested.

The room occupied the best part of the small bungalow. High-roofed, it housed looms, a spinning-wheel, a design table; the shelves lining the walls were crammed with wool. Deciding that she needed Tony's help in sorting out a further supply of goods for Ramon, Inez waved an expansive hand and invited Tessa to take a look round.

In turn, she inspected a small bedroom, a primitive kitchen, an outside loo, and a lean-to shack containing a bunk bed, the one time shelter of both shepherd and sheep, in inclement weather.

Returning to the studio Tessa, came upon Inez filling a sack with scarves to be taken back to Santa Fé. Supper, they must stay to supper, she insisted. Tony speedily accepted the invitation, and she hurried to her kitchen. Soon, the spicy aroma of simmering beef and chillis scented the hogan.

Meanwhile, the air outside had grown heavy, the sky dull. A strong breeze starting up, Tony and Tessa moved in from the patio and crowded into a corner of the kitchen.

The meal took an age to cook, dish after dish being

added to the menu, apéritif after apéritif being poured. Watching through a small window, Tessa grew perturbed; dark clouds were gathering. What time did their last connection to Santa Fé leave Taos, she enquired.

Airily, Inez waved a wooden spoon. There was no need to hurry, the buses ran late. But why worry? Why not stay the night?

Politely, Tessa declined the offer. Her sister might need her, her brother-in-law could grow concerned, she pointed out. The hogan lacking a phone, she couldn't advise her whereabouts.

At long last, the food was finally served, with not a little ceremony. To her dismay, Tessa found the chilli con carne too highly spiced to enjoy; the peppery sauce seared her mouth, sent tears to her eyes. Maddeningly, the other two diners ate with relish, Tony managing to finish his portion. The pancakes that followed could have been fried cowhide, they were so leathery, but while Tessa discreetly pushed hers to one side her companions chewed their helpings noisily. Her spirits sank, theirs soared.

When, oh when, would they get away? The familiarity she was forced to witness made her feel a complete outsider, and she couldn't wait to escape. The banging of a shutter against a wall, a sudden howl of wind, prompted her to urge their departure.

Eventually, they made it. A few yards from the hogan they felt a sprinkling of rain. At first a light drizzle, it had thickened to a downpour by the time they reached the plaza. Sheltering beneath the porch of a hotel, they waited for the bus.

The minutes passed and Tessa started to shiver.

'I hope the coach won't be much longer,' she said, through chattering teeth.

A waiter had appeared in the doorway and was peering hopefully out in search of clients. He flapped a dingy napkin.

'No more transportation through here tonight, lady,'

he said. 'You folk left it kind of late. Thirty minutes back, you'd have been okay.'

They checked; the information proved all too correct.

'It's your fault, Tony!' Tessa was taut with temper. 'I kept reminding you, kept urging we should leave, but you and your precious friend couldn't be hurried, could you?'

'Don't start brainstorming! There's no cause to get riled.' Tony's voice was calm, dead level. 'Inez'll be happy to put us up. We should've agreed, when she asked.'

He went to take her arm; angrily, she shrugged off his touch.

In fraught silence, they set off to retrace their steps. No sooner were they out of reach of houses, out of reach of shelter, than the storm vented its full force. Peal upon peal of thunder blasted their ears; streak upon streak of zig-zagging lightning blinded their eyes; monsoon-fierce, the rain lashed at them, stinging Tessa's skin, drenching her hair, soaking her cotton dress, saturating her sandals.

Seething with indignation, she picked a muddy path between lively puddles and tried not to stumble in the holes pocketing the dirt road. Why couldn't Tony learn to heed the passing of time, to live in the real world?

Inez betrayed not the slightest surprise at their return. Collecting cushions and blankets she made for the lean-to, announcing that she'd prepare the bunk bed. Offering to lend a hand, Tony followed on. A borrowed shawl over her goose-pimpled shoulders, Tessa crouched over the dying kitchen fire and endeavoured to towel-dry her hair. What a place to spend the night!

A rumble of low-pitched conversation wafted through the connecting doorway. Exchanging conspiratorial smiles, the bed-makers returned. Slipping an arm round Tessa, Tony drew her into the studio.

'What d'you know?' His lips touched one frozen ear. 'Inez insists she'll take the bunk, give up her own room.'

'But that wouldn't be fair,' Tessa protested. 'That bed

in there's adequate for two. I can easily share . . .'

'That's the idea,' he broke in. He pressed her to him. 'We'll be together in there, and Inez'll doss down in the lean-to. That way, sweetie, I can make you warm, hold you close all night, show you how much I love you.'

He ran his fingers down her spine. 'It's right, it's natural, for us to sleep together.'

For one long moment she was aware of the thud of his heart, the pleasing heat of his body, the comfort of his arms. Chilled to the bone, damp, weary, she longed to be held, fondled, cossetted. Cut off by the storm, isolated in the hogan, why not make the best of their predicament? But then, wasn't it Tony who'd brought it upon them, who'd landed them back in this primitive place? If he'd not dawdled, they'd be well on their way home. She could have enjoyed a hot bath, her own soft bed, clean clothes on waking.

Fury flooded through her and came to her rescue, bringing with it a suspicion, a fear. Could this stop-over have been planned? Deliberately contrived? Given Inez's cloying adoration, her craven desire to please Tony, it was possible . . .

Teeth grating, she pushed hard against him, pushed with all her might.

'Let me go! Get away!' she cried. 'Take your hands off me, you—you Casanova!'

The dark head violently jerked, the mane of black hair swung back, the gipsy eyes rounded in hurt.

'Tessa—Tessa, sweetie, do be reasonable! Please . . .' he pleaded, as she wrenched herself free. 'Please come back . . .'

But she was already slamming the door, the door of Inez's room, shooting bolt into socket. Trembling from head to foot, she threw herself against it, and only drew it open on receiving an assurance from Inez that she was alone outside and that she alone would come in.

Not speaking, not looking at each other, they left early next morning. Overnight, the rain had run itself out, leaving a clear azure sky, adobe walls gleaming like silk.

After the stuffiness of the hogan the washed air was like wine. Tessa's night had been far from restful; bed-sharing with the bulky Inez had meant clinging to an edge, an enforced audition of sonorous snores. Irked by the lack of personal toiletries, the absence of a shower, Tessa felt ill-kempt in her crumpled dress and still-damp sandals; she was in no mood to talk. Chin and cheeks wearing a twenty-four hour shadow, clothes creased, Inez's sack on his back, Tony looked more tramp than artist.

For more than half the journey they sat silent in the bus. Gradually, Tony eased his broad frame along the bench seat, covered Tessa's hand with his palm, murmured soft words of apology. Eyes tear-bright, voice thick with emotion, he begged forgiveness.

His genuine sorrow, his pleading tone, melted the ice in Tessa's heart, stirring compassion. Inez was the one to blame, she decided; it must have been her idea to bed them together. Bashful, shy, Tony would never have thought up the idea without prompting; no-one as honest as he would have secretly pre-planned the stay. Sudden temptation, that was what had lead to the proposition.

Far too fatigued for further fight, she sighed wearily, gave a slight nod and rested her head against his broad shoulder. Forgive and forget, that was the only way.

Near the central plaza, they descended from the bus. Santa Fé was awhirl with rush hour traffic; long queues of vehicles waited at the cross-road signals. Watching for the green light to shine her way, Tessa's gaze travelled from car to car, and she said a little prayer. Please let none of Mari's smart friends be around to see us, to report our untidy appearance.

The window of a cream sedan shot down, a blonde head peered out to check the length of the line ahead. Frowning, the driver directed her attention to the side walk, widened her green eyes. From the top of Tessa's ruffled hair down to her lack-lustre shoes they swept, then up again slowly. Every wrinkle in her dress they took in, before moving on to closely examine Tony's storm-stained denims.

Tessa caught her breath. Debra Petersen, of all people! Of all the rotten luck! After the ghastly night, this was all she needed. The crossing traversed, she bade Tony a hasty farewell.

Back at 'Los Arboles' she found a note from Ramon on her bed.

'Call me when you land back, I'd like to know you're OK' it read. 'Soonest pos. Mari'd like to see you. Trust you had a good time.'

It took a piping hot bath, a hair wash, a spotless dress, a meticulous grooming, before she could bring herself to lift the phone and to face the world.

Water-lily fresh, swathed in magnolia tulle, Marigold was stretched out on a chaise-longue when Tessa arrived to see her. She lifted a languid hand.

'Hi! Where've you been? Ramon sounded concerned when he called at breakfast-time. Said you'd not been home all night. You stayed in Taos? With one of Tony's pals?' The blonde brows arched. 'So, how was our budding artist?'

'I wish you'd not call him that!' Tessa tightened her lips. 'And don't go getting ideas. I shared a bed with friend Inez, Tony took the shepherd's bunk.'

'Hard luck on the shep.—and the sheep! My sweet, there's no call to look so po-faced.' She spread her hands. 'Who am I to worry—you're a big girl now! But take care how far you go with our Tony, don't let this get to a regular thing. There are differences, big differences, between you two.'

She examined her nails. 'He's fantastically attractive, that's for sure, but his world's not our world. He went to a mission school, did you know? And his family, such as it was, was church mouse poor.'

The blood rushed to Tessa's cheeks. Typical of Mari. What had happened, or might have happened, last night didn't matter; status and money did. Had she forgotten their own ordinary beginnings?

She drew herself tall. 'Thank you, I'll choose my own friends. Now, what was so urgent that it couldn't wait?'

Marigold blinked, then passed her a scribbled list.

'There's some shopping . . . Oh, Tess, don't look so cross!' Her mouth drooped. 'You don't know what it's like to be shut up here day after day, week after week. If only Blair'd see reason, let me come home . . .' A tear trembled on her lashes, rolled down one cheek.

Filled with remorse, Tessa hurried to her sister, slipped an arm round her.

'I'm sorry,' she murmured. 'It's easy to forget . . . freedom and health, we take them for granted until they're lost.'

She stroked the blonde curls. 'Nothing lasts forever, remember, not even pregnancy! Think of the lovely baby you're going to have, that'll be your reward. Now, how about a game of scrabble? First, though, I'll ring Wilma, and order you something special for supper.'

Until it was time for Marigold to take her afternoon rest, Tessa kept her company, then set off to do the shopping. Blair Lachlan's door stood ajar, and as she passed she heard Debra Petersen's voice.

'And there they were, eight-thirty this morning, looking for all the world like a pair of hobos.' Distinctly, the words floated out into the vestibule. 'The Taos bus was pulling away—they'd obviously ridden in on it. Heavy-eyed they looked, exhausted. What's the betting they'd been on a dirty weekend?'

There was a rustle of paper. 'Call it feminine intuition, knowledge of character, what you will, but right from the moment I set eyes on her, I knew it in my bones. That sister of Marigold Ruiz, I just knew she was that kind of girl!'

CHAPTER FIVE

'IF I were you, I'd not give the beastly insinuation a second thought,' Rosita counselled. Thoroughly upset by what she'd overheard, Tessa had opened her heart to her friend. 'Who is Mrs P. anyway? Nothing more than a jumped up desk clerk! From what little Dr Sep's let drop about the clinic staff, he doesn't rate her highly. And that kind of cattiness shouldn't impress Blair Lachlan; slander damages the one who speaks it, as much as it does the one spoken of, if not more. What matters is that your own conscience is clear.'

Suddenly, Rosita was a tower of strength.

'Oh, I do hope you're right,' Tessa muttered. No way did she wish to sink once again in the doctor's estimation.

Rosita shifted restlessly in her chair.

'You've not noticed any change, any difference, in me?'

Tessa concentrated her gaze. People! Why was it they inevitably wanted to turn attention to themselves?

'No-ooo . . .' She was puzzled. 'A clue, can you give me one?'

In answer Rosita pointed to her legs, raised her feet an inch or two.

'How about that, then? Remarkable, don't you think? That much progress, after only two treatments? Sep found a super physio.' Her eyes shone.

Tessa shook herself. How selfish could one get? Sunk deep in introspection, blinded by self-pity, she'd missed noticing the glow on the invalid's cheeks, her air of suppressed excitement.

'That's great, really great!' She grasped Rosita's hand.

'What a fantastic start! Mind you keep up the good work, carry on the exercises.'

Rosita chuckled. 'No doubts there, not with Santa Fé's answer to Dustin Hoffman around.'

'Who?' Tessa queried. 'A man?' She'd expected the para-medic to be a woman. Clever old Sep, she thought. Even if the treatment were only a placebo, a pledge of interest, it was pleasing Rosita and showed signs of working. Tessa was very glad, but she tempered her pleasure with caution. It was early days; too much mustn't be expected too soon.

Rosita was eyeing the distant mountains.

'Soon, perhaps, I'll be able to get into those hills. What do you think Sep's planning—a special outing for a few people like me, a pinon picking barbecue. This time of year, folk collect up pine nuts to use in New Mexican food. With him along and in charge, I'd not feel so nervous.

'But you've not yet told me about your trip up to Taos—what did you think of it? Your uncomfortable night, yes, I've heard about that, but not about your impressions of the place.'

'Dreamy, I thought it,' Tessa hurried to say. 'I could imagine Indian braves there and frontiersmen.'

'Mm-mm.' Rosita agreed. 'One of our favourite spots, it used to be, for picnics en famille. We'd ride horseback from the estancia and laze beside a waterfall while Rae and Papa went fishing for trout. Later on, we'd drive up in a gang, boys and girls together, and have a cook-out . . .' Her voice faded; unseeing, she gazed into the distance.

The man she'd sent away, had he been one of the number? Tessa sought a diplomatically phrased question. Before she could find words, Conchita came bustling in. Full of praise for the new physio, she burbled brightly about her daughter's slight progress.

The matter occupied Tessa's mind as she made her way to Tony's studio for her second portrait sitting. She felt a certain responsibility for the resumption of the treatment. If it succeeded, it would be wonderful, but what if it failed? The thought of the disillusion, the unhappiness, that would follow was daunting.

She wasn't too certain, either, that Debra Petersen's allegation would be totally ignored; 'no smoke without fire' might be one reaction. Why the antagonism? She had done nothing to deliberately upset the secretary.

Tony betrayed little concern on hearing of the incident. 'So what?' He hunched his shoulders. 'We know what this dame implied isn't true, though if I'd had my way . . .' His lips twisted in a wry smile. 'Anyway, what we choose to do is no business of Lachlan's, his secretary, anyone's. There's always some mischief-maker around, waiting to make a mountain out of a molehill, a scandal out of a suspicious circumstance. Take no notice! What I strongly object to is the label 'dirty' being applied to a night spent 'a deux'. I see nothing dirty about a man longing to possess a woman, a woman wanting a man.' He cast her a hungry look.

'The portrait,' she said hurriedly. 'You're ready for the session? Let me run a comb through my hair.'

Blair Lachlan's opinion mightn't matter to Tony, she thought, tugging out a small tangle, but it did matter to her. She wasn't keen to acquire that kind of reputation and didn't want to be thought an easy lay. What in the world had possessed La Petersen?

Marigold had an answer.

'I'd say it was obvious,' she declared. 'Jealousy, that's what it is! Somewhere along the SF grapevine she's learned that Blair partnered you at the dance she'd passed up, had a great time. Old green eyes doesn't miss a trick, I did warn you. And talking of parties, I've an invitation to pass on to you.'

She handed Tessa a gilt-edged card engraved in copper plate. 'From Anna—strictly informal this affair, ordinary gear. Drinks and food on the patio, swimming after. The Emerys'll send a car for you, like before. This time, Anna's making sure you get the invite and details

in writing. Just wait till you see their pool—it's Holly-
wood down to the last tile, with separate kitchen and
bar. You being a good swimmer you should have a great
evening.'

She cupped her chin in her hands. 'How long, dear
heaven, how long, before I can take a dip? Right now,
I'd look like an inflated sack! How I envy you! How the
days drag. You'll have to cope with all the baby shopping, I fear, and get the spare room fitted as a nursery. If
Blair doesn't soon let me out for a breather, I'll have to
step up my "Release Ruiz" campaign.

The violet eyes slid to the invitation card.

'Could be you'll meet Blair again, at the swim-in.'

'You think so? You really believe DP'll let him go
free?'

'Have to, won't she, if she's not asked? We'll have to
wait and see.'

Would he, wouldn't he, be there? Her peacock blue
and green caftan would class as informal, worn with blue
sandals, and she'd take her candy-stripe bikini along too.
She'd be the soul of discretion, not mention the party to
Tony, or anyone; there was no need. A fun evening, a
'one-off', she didn't intend it to disrupt her regular
dating.

The Emery property was a ranch in Spanish style and
lay in a wide valley some four miles from Santa Fé.
Rose-walled, round arched, the four-square building
was centred by a fountained courtyard.

A score or so of guests stood grouped by the splashing
water when Tessa arrived. One quick glance and she was
reassured; this time, she had donned the correct
uniform, the rig of the day. Many of the men, as well as
most of the women, had put on caftans. One exception
stood out head and shoulders above the rest of the
company, his safari suit the colour of café-au-lait, his
polo-neck shirt silky black.

'Good to see you, Tessa Maitland,' Blair said, amber
eyes twinkling down. Smiling her pleasure, Tessa
wondered why he called her by both her names, why she

found the habit so attractive. Swiftly, her gaze darted over the other female guests: not one ash-blonde! She felt a spasm of joy; the evening was going to be super. A change was as good as a rest.

The saying proved true. They dined out on the terrace, but she didn't remember what they ate. They chatted, but she had only a hazy recollection of what they said. They assisted in the selection of tapes to click into the cassette player, but the tunes didn't register. She was only aware of him, his towering slim frame, lean handsome face.

And suddenly there they were, swimming together in the moonlit pool, splashing diamonds of water at every stroke, plunging, diving, racing. As competitors they were well matched; Tessa was quicker off the mark, Blair had the greater staying power. Time and time again they pitted their skill and in between they rested against the blue-tiled edge to get back their breath. Her body close to his, separated by only the flimsiest of bikinis, the narrowest of briefs, she was very conscious of his strength.

The night grew chill, and they went off to dress, hurrying back. She found herself racing along the path to rejoin him.

'May I see you home?' He asked what she'd been willing him to ask. Beside him in the streamlined Porsche, she felt as if she hadn't a care in the world. Nestling back, she closed her eyes, hummed in tune to the sentimental Sinatra number floating from the dashboard radio. Such a night were dreams made of . . .

The powerful car slid to a smooth halt. Slowly, Tessa opened her eyes, lifted her head. What she saw made her jerk straight in her seat. Instead of the apartment block she gazed on a lone adobe bungalow framed in tall pines, instead of the plate glass entrance a heavily carved Spanish-style door, lit by a swinging lantern. Beneath the wide porch stood a small green Ford.

She stared. 'But—but this isn't "Los Arboles"!'

He gave a wide grin. 'No! This is "Los Pinos".'

She knitted her brow. 'You said—you said you were driving me home . . .'

'That is correct, and I never tell a lie. Washington is my middle name.' Leaning over, he clicked open her door. 'Which is, dear Tessa Maitland, exactly what I have done. Surely you realised? It was my home I meant, not yours!'

Tense, rigid, she stayed in her seat. Even when he'd walked round the car and arrived at her side, she made no attempt to stir. The arrogance, the conceit!

'You don't imagine I'm going to get out, come in there with you?' Indignation shrilled her voice.

'And why not? I'd like you to meet my mother, and for her to meet you. That's her car over there, so I know she's arrived back from her bridge date. And she must still be up—the lights are all on.'

Every window shone bright. Curious, Tessa ran her gaze the breadth of the long row. Outside, the house was delightful; but what was it like inside? And what was Mrs Lachlan like? Did her son resemble her, in any way?

He stood holding back the door.

'Why the hesitation? Are you chicken?' The heavy lids hooded the hawk-like eyes. 'Now, if it were Arretino standing here, you'd not be that slow.'

That did it. Promptly, she swung from her seat.

'Ten minutes then, and not a single second more!' She held up a cautionary finger. 'It's nearly midnight, and I've still to get home, thanks to this detour. You should've asked, before bringing me out of my way.'

'I did!' Chuckling, he took her arm. 'No fault of mine, that you didn't read the message right. Wait while I let you in.'

They went into a small hall, descended a short flight of stairs and entered a large living-room. Tessa looked on parchment coloured walls, a beamed ceiling, Persian rugs spread on a polished floor. Velvet the shade of gentians curtained the recessed windows, books filled the plethora of shelves, paintings and drawings hung in well arranged groups. Though sparse, the furniture was elegantly comfortable—a pair of button-back chairs flanked the brick fireplace, a coffee table centred matching settees. There was a bureau-desk, a Spanish bridal chest, a music centre beneath a cover of smoked glass. The setting was gracious but not opulent, decorative but not ornate, the style neither old nor modern. It was her kind of room, her kind of home.

'Your mother's not here . . .' She looked at Blair.

'She'll be around.' He went to the door. 'Lenore!' he called, and again, 'LENORE!' Cocking his head, he stood listening. The house stayed silent.

'Find a seat while I go take a look.' He gestured to the nearer settee. He went out and she saw him cross the hall, disappear, heard his footfall along a corridor. His voice echoed back: 'Mother! Moth—er! Lenore!' The steps grew loud again. Returning, he shook his head, shut the door.

'Might as well try to waken the dead—Ma's out for the count, I took a squint through into her room. She must've got back earlier than usual. You must meet another time.'

He waved a hand towards the low table. 'Coffee? There's a thermos on the tray. You pour, while I deal with the fire. No cream for me.'

Kicking a log into life, he tossed on fir cones from a basket. Flames leapt high, a fragrant scent came wafting.

'That's better,' he said. 'Now we shan't need all these lights.' Going from lamp to lamp, he turned all of them out save one, and that he dimmed by moving the switch.

Tessa had filled the coffee cups, had settled against the velvet cushions. The soft light, the flickering fire, the pleasant warmth, had a relaxing effect, after the energetic swimming. The apprehension she'd originally felt vanished from her mind.

Sinking down beside her, Blair nodded round. 'We've got it just right; I call this real cosy.'

One sip of coffee and he was on his feet again. 'There's one thing missing—music, we must have some music.'

'Debussy, do you like Debussy?' he enquired, from the music centre. 'Claire de Lune, how about that?'

Softly, the sweet strains trembled the air, and he returned to the settee. Swelling in volume, the music grew loud.

'Your mother, this noise—it won't disturb her?' Tessa asked.

'Not a chance!' He grinned, and she thought how very white his teeth were. 'The last trump wouldn't rouse Lenore, not once Morpheus has her in his grasp. Turn the sound down if you wish; I'm not getting up again!'

'Charming!' Tessa went over, lowered the control. By the time she got back he'd stretched out his long legs.

'Move!' she ordered. 'I want to get to my seat.'

'Step high, and you can!'

She lifted her foot, he shifted his legs, at one and the same time. Her feet went slipping from under her. Trying to regain her balance, she threw out both hands, went crashing down.

Firm hands grasped her, steadied her, swung her round.

'So, a perfect knee landing, Tessa Maitland! Ah-hah, so now we can get properly acquainted . . .' His tone, at first jocular, thickened, his words slowed; he tightened his hold.

'Delicious, you feel delicious!' Fiercely, he nuzzled his chin against her cheek, tilted her face, covered her mouth with his mouth. She felt his heart pound, heard his breath grow heavy. His kiss, hard, bruising, set her tingling with desire, desire such as she'd never known. His mouth sought on, his hands explored; all resistance ebbed from her . . .

Air, she must have air. She twisted her head, tried to struggle away. 'I can't breathe . . .'

He let her go, threw back his head, inhaled. 'There, surely that was proof? I make a better lover, wouldn't you say? Admit it! Admit that I outdo that splasher of paint!' His breath came in long gasps. 'Don't pull away, don't pretend you don't like me! Your lips betrayed you!

Arretino, you spared an entire night; me, I ask only for one hour!'

Her anger flamed. The arrogance! The conceit!

'You—you brute! Debra Petersen, how about her . . . ?'

There was a creak, the creak of a floor-board, a muffled step. The door rattled, the knob turned. Desperately, Tessa attempted to slide down from the high knee. A light voice came floating in.

'Blair, dear, is that you? I heard a noise—came to make sure . . .'

A wraith-like form stepped from the shadows. Tessa caught the outline of a slim figure, a long robe.

'Oh! I didn't realise . . . You're not alone . . . Excuse me!'

Swivelling on her slippered heels, Mrs Lachlan fled, full skirt billowing behind her.

Like statues they sat, poker erect, gaze fixed ahead, all the way to 'Los Arboles'.

At the entrance Blair Lachlan jumped from the Porsche, threw back the passenger door.

'A pity, that disappointing finale,' he drawled, as Tessa climbed out. 'The interruption was, to say the least, unfortunate. Doomed we seem, over-ruled by fate . . .'

Lifting a hand, he smoothed his cheek, touched the line of the white scar. In spite of her wrath, Tessa knew a stab of compassion.

'Adios!' He gave a short bow, a click of heels. Shoulders squared, he marched back to the car, drove off.

Watching till the rear lights, glinting like angry red eyes, had disappeared, Tessa felt an icy finger trace her spine. What a disaster, what a humiliation! No evening could have had a better beginning, a worse ending. To be caught in flagrante delicto . . . ! What could Mrs Lachlan have thought? Met again, would she be recognised?

Furious, vexed with herself, she clenched her fists. How stupid, how fool-hardy, she'd been, allowing the doctor to entice her into his home, acting the fly to the spider.

Adding insult to injury, not a word of apology had he offered, not the slightest sign of remorse had he shown. But then, he was hardly the type to ever admit transgression, to ask forgiveness. Self-important, self-satisfied, it wasn't surprising he'd had to wait so long to find someone to marry.

Right from the moment Tessa arrived in the studio, Tony was off-hand, moody. His reply to her greeting was unusally curt, the smile that edged his lips didn't reach his eyes.

Endeavouring not to show her disappointment, Tessa took up her position on the model's throne. Obliquely, she watched him out of the corner of an eye. Why so out of temper, so withdrawn? What had happened? Such behaviour was totally out of character. Though never garrulous, he had a habit of gently babbling as he worked, making small talk. It was his method, she suspected, of setting sitters at their ease, of gaining insight into character.

Square to his easel he stood, splashing paint on canvas. Blair Lachlan's jibe went through her mind; what an ignoramus! Outside medicine, the man didn't understand anyone, anything; certainly, he was totally unable to appreciate Tony's talent.

A gloomy hush hung over the studio, a dullness not helped by an unexpected clouding of the sky; the light creeping through the windows was smoke grey. Mercifully, it blanketed the squalor; less kindly, it helped to deepen the atmosphere of depression.

Ill at ease, Tessa twisted a fraction on her chair; crisply, she was requested to keep still.

At long last the mid-way break arrived. Tossing down palette and brush, Tony ripped open two cans of Coke and handed one to her.

'You liked the Emery place?' He clipped his words. 'Wheeler-dealing, that's the way they acquired that fine hacienda.'

Her jaw dropped. How had he come to hear? Mari must've told Rae. But why had Rae passed on the information?

'The house is lovely.' She chose to ignore the comment. 'You've visited there?'

'What, me?' He stabbed a finger at his chest. 'Do I look socio-economic Class A? I've only seen it from the road. That swim-pool complex sticks out like Remembrance Garden monument; it's too new, too ugly, for that lovely old house. But there, what else can you expect from folk like that? You—You had fun?'

'Why, yes—but I . . .'

'And Doc Lachlan, he was there?'

She stiffened. An inspired guess, or hound-dog trailing?

'Among others. That's not surprising—he is a friend of the Emerys.'

'Oh, yes? Seems like you two are being thrown together quite a bit, of late.' His scowl was ugly.

'Twice, to be precise.' She sucked in her breath. 'You don't have to look so suspicious. His secretary may have plenty going for him, but I see him as the original male chauvinist!'

The coal-black eyes pierced into hers; she managed to retain a steady gaze. The tautness left his body.

'If you're ready, we'll get back to work.' He spoke calmly.

The second half of the session was comfortably relaxed; Tessa observed that Tony painted with a freer hand, that he no longer furrowed his brow. Sitting quietly with time to think, she pondered on what she owed him. He had given her confidence, appreciation, time; to Tony, she was indebted for most of the happiness she'd found in Santa Fé. Kind and thoughtful, he'd always been on hand when needed; generous to a fault, he'd risked Ramon's ire by painting her portrait. Poor darling, it wasn't fair that he'd been made jealous. The end of the sitting found her swamped in sympathy, understanding, affection.

She hugged him when he lifted her from the dais, stroked his forehead.

'You look much better, now that black bear has vanished from your shoulder. The one who brings bad black moods, I mean,' she went on to explain, noting his puzzlement.

Amusement lit his eyes.

'My dear sweet, my dear crazy Tessa!' He linked his arms behind her back, gazed adoringly. 'I can't help the way I feel. You know me, you know the way it is. I'm a one-girl guy.'

Blissfully, she surrendered to his caress. Heaven, it was, to be wanted, and not just taken for granted.

Fine, golden for the most part, the October days slid by. To everyone's relief, Marigold's condition continued to improve. The oedema decreased, leaving ankles and fingers slender once more, her blood pressure lowered to near normal, headaches ceased. The one thing that didn't get any better was her attitude to the clinic. On the contrary, her greater strength gave greater energy for fault finding. Not a single omission was overlooked, not a minute's delay tolerated.

'Inefficiency's something one must never put up with,' she stressed, repeatedly. 'That way, service only deteriorates, value's not received for money spent. This I learnt as an air hostess. When delays occurred, it was the pushy passengers who got priority, the quiet little people were left behind. All the time, I saw it. Here, they've a saying that sums it up, "Nice guys finish last!"'

Tessa recalled a few of the more difficult patients she'd nursed and recognised there was some truth in what her sister said. But she couldn't agree, not entirely. In hospital, at any rate, persistent grumblers eventually got their come-uppance, usually. Privately, she decided her sister was convalescent tetchy.

Less satisfactorily, Rosita's progress had levelled out, had reached a plateau. Her legs had become less flabby and, sitting, she could raise her feet a distance from the ground, but she still lacked the confidence to even try to stand.

'There seems little point in going on with treatment,' she told Tessa dejectedly. 'Let's face it—Does it matter whether or not I get to walk? I've managed long enough as I am. My physio, though, is adamant that I will continue.'

Good for him, Tessa thought. The good-looking paramedic, could it be he had a personal reason, in addition to a professional one, for the insistence? Having met him and observed the admiring attention he paid his pretty patient, she found herself wondering. A bachelor, well-established in a thriving practice, he was eligible as a husband. The fact that he'd been unable to arouse the slightest interest from Rosita confirmed Tessa's conviction that it was for her long lost lover that the invalid yearned, no-one else.

If only the man could be found . . . Free still and still attracted, able to accept Rosita as she was, he could be reinstated in the role of the suitor. Otherwise, it was better that she knew the truth, learn to adjust, eventually dismiss him from mind.

Meanwhile, the challenge was there. How to discover more about him, learn his name, his whereabouts? Who to ask? Not Rosita, for she avoided direct questions; not Conchita, for she might get upset. Marigold knew nothing, she'd already discovered, and had been totally unaware of any long-term romance; Ramon had revealed all he knew. Who else was there?

One possibility suddenly occurred to Tessa as she went to step into the clinic elevator one afternoon, on her way up to visit Marigold. Stethoscope garlanded, Dr Sepulveda was bustling about. Seeing her he stopped, asked her how she was, and the thought hit, wasn't Sep the very person? Hadn't he know the Ruiz for years, been a friend, as well as a medical adviser? A moment's hesitation, and she made the request. Could he spare a few minutes to discuss a mutual acquaintance? Should she make an appointment?

Quizzically, the beady eyes stared, then he waved towards his office.

'Come with me,' he invited. 'For young ladies— attractive young ladies—I can always find time. Anyway, my coffee recess is due, and I'm sure we can find an extra cup.'

Motioning Tessa to an armchair, he waddled to the other side of an imposing desk and threw down his stethoscope. Behind him hung a large wall placard: 'NO SMOKING! SMOKING IS A HAZARD TO HEALTH!' Flicking the notice a baleful glance, the doctor slid open a top drawer and fished out two cellophaned packs. Extracting a cigar from one, a match from the other, he lit up, puffed hard, gave a seraphic smile, and arranged his bulky form on a swivel chair.

Chins tucked in, head lowered, he regarded Tessa over the rim of his spectacles.

'Rosita, what is it you wish to know about her?'

'You—guessed?' The opening came as a relief to Tessa; there was no need to delay or feel her way. In she plunged, told of her ideas concerning the invalid and her hopes; finally, she put the all important question.

Lazaro Sepulveda listened closely, moving only to tap ash into the open drawer. When she'd finished speaking he didn't make a reply. Instead, he got up, crossed to a steel cabinet, started fumbling inside.

'Ros' records,' he said, taking out a file and holding it high. 'To refresh my memory.' He tapped his balding head. 'Most of the details I have lodged in here, but to be certain . . .'

Regaining his seat, he rustled through the papers.

'Ah yes, I think I have the complete picture now. This man of whom you speak, Alvaro and Con came to see me about him, when a marriage seemed in the offing and wanted to know if I thought him a fair health risk. The beau himself, I never got to meet, but Rosita I've known all her life. Of course, I brought her into this world. Twenty-one, no, twenty-two years ago. Dear me, how time flies. It doesn't seem possible . . .'

Puffing out a smoke ring, he studied it reflectively. Eager though she was for information, Tessa didn't dare break his chain of thought. He swivelled his chair.

'Where were we? Ah, yes, Rosita's beau. You've gathered, maybe, that he didn't meet with parental approval? Nothing against him, mark you—he simply wasn't the sort of fellow they'd hoped for, they'd been accustomed to knowing.'

Tessa leant forward. 'His name,' she prompted. 'Do you remember his name? Where he lived? Where he worked?'

The doctor lunged forward, seizing the house phone.

'Coffee—I forgot about our coffee!' Leaving Tessa on the edge of her chair, he reminded someone he was in his office, and thirsty.

'Nope!' Recradling the receiver, he shook his head. 'I never did know his name, Al and Con didn't say and I didn't enquire. A doctor learns not to ask unnecessary questions, to save his breath for the essentials. And Al was already quite sick, he didn't want bothering. Anyway, this guy was persona non grata, by that time; he and Ros were going it alone. Where he worked, yes, that I did learn. Up at Los Alamos—Atomic City, to you and me. His was a world of science, the Ruiz was one of the soil—no common ground, you see. Strange, the details that get filed away in the old grey matter. That did, and his limp.'

'His—limp?' Tessa gulped. It couldn't be true! 'He had a limp? How old would he be? Were you able to gather his age?' The questions came in a rush.

'Late twenties, I'd say—yes, eight years or so older than Rosita; that I do remember because the poliomyelitis he'd suffered dated from an epidemic, and that's how he came by that gammy leg.' My dear old friends were worried it could be handed on, if he and Ros married. On that point, I was able to reassure them.'

A tap came on the door. With one sweep of his hand, the little doctor thrust the cigar inside the drawer, stubbed it out, and slammed the drawer shut. Windmilling his arms at the haze of smoke, he growled 'Come in!'

'Oh, it's only our coffee—I thought it might be my next patient.' He signalled for the porter to put the tray on the desk and breathed a sigh of relief.

'How far did I get—yes, the lameness. Ironic, wasn't it? There they were, those two doting parents, worried sick over a minor handicap, and poor Ros ended up in a wheelchair. I've often wondered about that . . .'

He tapped the side of his nose. 'Everything I've told you is between ourselves, strictly confidential. Anything else you wish to know?'

Her heart in her mouth, Tessa had difficulty framing the question, the question she was bursting to ask. Like a jigsaw lacking its final section, the Identikit picture she'd been building in her mind awaited completion.

The man she'd run into at Albuquerque was a scientist employed at Los Alamos and he'd looked around thirty. And hadn't he worked a previous contract in New Mexico, made friends in the State, friends with whom he'd since lost touch?

The similarities were staggering.

She gripped the edge of the desk.

'The man you've been speaking of—did you ever get to hear the colour of his hair?' she asked. 'Do you know if it was—red?'

CHAPTER SIX

WINGS, Tessa might have been on, not in an elevator, as she went soaring up to Marigold's floor. Inwardly, she was still chuckling at Dr Sepulveda's start of surprise at her final question.

'Red hair? *Red* hair?' he'd asked. 'Does that necessarily go with a limp?'

Mouth gaping, he'd stared as if she'd gone out of her mind, but had laughed on hearing her explanation. No, he'd never heard tell of the beau's colouring, but he wished her joy in her search. And he'd agreed wholeheartedly that nothing better for Rosita could happen, than that her lover should return.

Tessa could have jumped for joy, and would have done so, but for the note of warning that sounded in her brain. Every clue so far obtained seemed to confirm that the man she'd met on the plane was Rosita's long lost suitor, but he still had to be traced, proved to be interested, and willing. And free! He hadn't *looked* married, hadn't mentioned a wife or family, but . . .

Much remained to be done. Los Alamos, she must get up to Los Alamos, as soon as possible.

Lightly, she tripped into her sister's room, then slowed her steps. The place had a different look. Suitcases were piled near the door, possessions had been stacked. And Mari wasn't sitting up propped against pillows, but lying completely flat. The outline of her figure beneath the quilt was all Tessa could see.

She held her breath. What had happened? A setback? Was Marigold worse. In long strides she reached the bed.

'Mari, it's Tess!' she said, twisting her hands. 'Are you—are you all right?'

A hand appeared on the quilt's upper edge, whisked it back. Jack-in-the-box quick, Marigold sat up, her face one big grin.

'Hi!' she said. 'Gave you a shock, did I? Well, you've only yourself to blame. What an age you've taken getting here! Hours, I've been waiting. Time and again, I've called the apartment; Wilma kept saying you were on your way. See, I'm dressed, rarin' to go.' She touched the lavender blouse she was wearing. 'Didn't expect to see me out of my nightie, did you?'

Tessa gaped. 'Raring to go where? And why are you dressed? I don't get it . . .'

Marigold clapped her hands. 'Blair's letting me out, that's what! Fantastic, isn't it? These last few days, he's been giving approving nods and grunts each time he checked me over, and this morning he did a head to toes job, pronounced me well enough to leave. I've to continue resting, of course, but it'll be heaven to get home.'

'Why, that's super!' Tessa said, beaming. 'Everything's coming right! I'm so glad for you. When do we leave?'

'Not till he's given you instructions—he said for you to go down and see him, the minute you arrived.'

The pleasure Tessa had been feeling oozed from her. A price, there was always a price to pay, for everything. Her knees went weak at the thought of facing the doctor, but she forced a smile. No way must she spoil things for Marigold.

'I'd better go now, I suppose, and get it over with.'

The violet eyes narrowed. 'You two at loggerheads again? After sharing a great time at Anna's? Got on like a house on fire, or was it hearts, that she said? Come to think of it, you never said a word about the "swim-in".'

'Haven't had a chance.' Tessa walked to the door and looked back. 'Heavens, what a shock you gave me, hiding, then leaping up like that!'

The shock had been two-fold. First, there'd been the fright of coming upon Marigold covered like a corpse; second, the news that she had to face Blair Lachlan.

Since the night he'd lured her into his home, they'd not met.

Marigold fluttered a hand. 'Oh, do get a move on! I want to get out of here, take a look at the outside world. Most of all, I want to get back to the apartment ahead of Rae and give him a surprise. Dear man, he deserves it.'

'You'd better report to the green-eyed dragon first,' she called after Tessa. 'That one's bound to be mounting guard.'

She was, bandbox neat as ever, not a bleached hair out of place. A nod of confimation that Tessa was expected, and she led her into the doctor's office.

The tall figure rose from behind his desk, jerked acknowledgement. Nervous, Tessa fingered the collar of her blue linen jacket and twitched the buckle of her belt to dead centre. Suddenly, she felt like a first year student being interviewed by a medical superintendent.

'Good afternoon, Miss Maitland, please take a seat.' His voice was all on one level, detached, cool.

Miss Maitland, indeed! Who was he trying to fool—her, himself, La Petersen? Her gaze slid to the secretary, and she was relieved to see her leave the office. Taking the chair indicated, she sat ramrod-stiff; the doctor remained standing.

'I'll not keep you long,' he said. 'You've heard I'm allowing your sister home? Two factors influenced my decision. One is that we've considerable pressure on our beds, a backlog of urgent cases. More important, Marigold's progressed sufficiently for her to be cared for at home. Her blood pressure's around 120/60, her urine's been free of albumin the last run of tests, and the oedema's reduced; she's feeling much better. At the moment there appears little cause for immediate anxiety.'

He cleared his throat. 'Even so, I'd not permit her to leave us but for one important consideration—that she's able to have the care and attention of a fully trained nurse. I take it you are willing to take full responsibility?'

The amber eyes seemed to pierce through her.

'Of course.' She gave a sharp nod. 'That was my suggestion, I seem to remember, in the first place.'

His eyebrows twitched. 'Listen to me, and listen carefully. Marigold is to be on strict bed-rest. Twice a day—I suggest one hour mid-morning, another late afternoon, she may move out on a chaise-longue on the balcony, providing the weather stays fine. All the time, she is to keep her feet level with her head. You will continue the treatment prescribed, give the drugs required in correct dosage. I've had a supply put ready, a schedule made out.'

He handed her a well-wrapped package.

'Starting tomorrow, I require a urine sample to be brought here every second day, for testing. About smoking—Marigold has cut it down, but I'd prefer to see it cut right out. Food—no over-indulgence, not too much protein or salt. And alcohol—that should be limited to an occasional glass of wine. Anything you wish to know?'

The question, abruptly delivered, made her start. Her heart was thudding in her ears. How could this man look so calm, so composed? Those taut lips, had they actually sought hers in a passionate kiss? Those cool hands, had they ardently caressed? The coldness, the indifference! She might well have been some unknown agency nurse, receiving instructions on a new case.

She stood up, straightened her shoulders. 'None that occur to me, right at this moment. I may call you, I take it, should the need arise?'

He nodded assent, tossed back the tawny curl that fell forward.

'Of course, and I'll be looking in, regularly. One thing more—above all else, watch out that Marigold doesn't get over-tired. My hope is that she'll be happier in her own home, more content. Here, I have to admit, she's not been the most amenable of patients. With care, I trust she'll carry till full term. If you have the slightest cause for concern, let me know immediately. My secretary'll give you a diet sheet, on your way out.'

His gaze met hers, lingered. She watched him run the tip of his tongue over wide red lips, the lips that had been so urgent, so searching, so demanding. For one split second, she thought he was about to murmur a pleasantry, abandon the strict formality. . . .

Instead, he marched to the door, opened it.

'I hand your sister into your charge, Nurse Maitland.' He proffered a hand that was icy, as cold as his voice.

The departure from the clinic was unforgettable. It took Tessa, Dagmar Fisher, two nursing aides, a small squad of porters, to bear out Marigold's suitcases, holdalls, carrier bags. In addition there were the unwieldy unpackables—a reading lamp with a long trailing wire, cartons of books and magazines, baskets filled with fruit, overflowing with knitting, sewing materials, games; a radio-cassette player. It was a ragged exodus.

Resignedly, Tessa helped pile the luggage into the Emerys' limousine, borrowed for the purpose. She'd seen it all before, this kind of carry-on. Too often, private patients tended to cart quantities of possessions into hospital with them. Sincerely they intended to occupy every waking minute; seldom did they manage to do much more than glance through a periodical.

With not a little relief she got her sister safely back to 'Los Arboles', and helped her get to bed.

'Now, see here, I insist that we start as we mean to go on,' she said, staff-nurse strict. 'For anything you want, no matter how trifling, how small, you ask me or Wilma; you are not to go hopping up and down, in and out, but stay resting, all the time. If you don't, you'll risk having your blood-pressure shoot up again, and a return to the LS. And that'd get us in bad books with you-know-who, the last thing either of us wishes. So long as you remember I'm in charge, you'll be all right. Is that understood?'

Meekly, Marigold gave her agreement. 'I'll do everything you say—I'm completely at your mercy, aren't I?

Oh, it's great being home—I can't wait to see Rae's face.'

It was one broad smile, when he set eyes on his wife.

'My darling, how marvellous . . .' His voice breaking, he took her in his arms, and Tessa hurried to leave them alone, saying that she must call Tony.

By phoning the gallery, she managed to contact him, give him the news. Explaining her new responsibilities she cried off her date with him that evening, warned that their time together would have to be curtailed, while Marigold needed nursing. As always he was sympathetic, understanding.

With Wilma, she planned and prepared a special 'Welcome Home' supper, and set a table beside Marigold's bed. As pleased as a puppy with two tails, Ramon bustled round waiting on his wife.

Tired but happy, Tessa settled for an early night. The knowledge that her sister was progressing satisfactorily had lifted a weight from her mind. In the space of a few hours the apartment had acquired a happier atmosphere, a different feel, and everyone was content. Though she was well aware that the increased demands upon her would leave little freedom, she wasn't worried; evenings and Sundays when Ramon was around, she'd be able to see Tony. Visits to Rosita would have to be less frequent, and her trip to Los Alamos postponed. The main thing was to look after Marigold.

Please, guide her to behave sensibly, she prayed: let her continue to improve, have an easy delivery, a healthy child.

The last thing she desired was to fail in her task. Blair Lachlan's disapproval was something she could well do without.

Marigold looked radiant, next morning. Enveloped in silky eau-de-nil chiffon, she sat supported by a small mountain of pillows while she had her breakfast, and scribbed several memos. One, she handed to Tessa.

'You'll be shopping for fresh fruit and veg?' she asked.

'Could you also get me the things on that note? Rae left a stack of cash on his dresser, should you need any.'

Tessa ran her eyes over the list.

'All these things? All these luxury foods?' She raised her brows. 'You do know the freezer's almost full, and the store cupboard? We've not exactly been eating you out of house and home, while you've not been here.'

Marigold tightened her lips. 'I'm going to have exactly what I fancy! It's all right for you—you've not been enduring hospital food. Okay, so you brought in special dishes, but by the time I got them the craving had left me. Pregnancy affects one that way.' She pointed to the sheet of paper. 'The items I've starred you'll find in the "Deli", the others in any "Cash and Carry".'

'Don't worry about me,' she called out, as Tessa reached the apartment door. 'I'm on Cloud Nine! Wilma's on hand, if I need anything.'

The shopping took an age. The delicatessen was crowded, and there were long queues at the supermarket check-out. Her arms crammed with crackling paper sacks, Tessa took a taxi back home, anxious to get there quickly. During her absence, had Marigold stayed resting, faithfully following instructions?

To her great relief, she found that she had. From her bedchair on the balcony, Marigold lifted a languid hand.

'Hi! Frightfully guilty you make me feel, when I see you looking all hot and bothered. I've been sloth-idle. I had Wilma bring the phone out here and spent the time ringing my buddies to advise my change of address. You didn't forget my Winstons?'

Handing over the multiple pack of cigarettes, Tessa shook her head in disapproval.

'I almost didn't buy them—you know you're supposed to ease up on smoking.'

'Oh, fooey!' Marigold smote the air. 'Heavens, I must do *something*. No sports, no walking, no fun, no games—life's very dull.'

Her pretty mouth drooped. 'You've no idea what it's like, having to be a cabbage. And, right now, I have a pressing problem, one I'm hoping you'll help me solve. With all these alarms and excursions, I've forgotten something terribly important. Do you know what to-morrow is?'

Tessa considered. 'You mean, apart from being Thursday?'

'I most certainly do! Rae—it's his birthday—imagine, he'll be thirty! And I've no present for him! How stupid can pregnancy make one? I hardly know what month it is, let alone the date. Thank heaven Conchita dropped by at coffee time, and reminded me. Usually I've some-thing ready, way ahead.'

Beseechingly, she looked at Tessa. 'You won't mind going back to town, this afternoon? That's darling of you! I'll make all this up to you, as soon as I'm out and about. The best tourist guide in New Mexico, I'll become—walk you till your feet drop off, drive you till you're car-sick!'

She rubbed her forehead. 'Now, what to get Rae? Aren't men difficult to buy for? Over lunch, I'll have a big think. Flowers, I'll want a lot of flowers, as well. I'll draw you a map of where to go.'

The meal over, she handed Tessa a sketch.

'Try Canyon Row, for the present,' she suggested. '"L'Italia" there stocks lovely silk goods—get some-thing gorgeous in the cravat line. Don't worry over-much about the design—they'll exchange, if it doesn't suit. And you don't have to rush, there's no need to hurry back. While you're gone, I'll put on a face-pack and take a siesta.'

She was lying stretched out on her bed, cheeks and brow covered in putty-coloured paste, when Tessa went to say goodbye.

'A mummy, that's what you look like,' Tessa re-marked. 'One of the Egyptian variety.'

'US, if you please,' the beige lips mumbled, in protest.

The afternoon being fine and bright, Tessa was happy to be out-of-doors, and she enjoyed the stroll along Canyon Row. An old-time Indian trail, it had developed into an artists' colony of shops mingled with houses. Galleries and studios abounded, and there were work-rooms galore. Glancing through doorways she could see coppersmiths and leatherworkers, weavers and glass-blowers, inspected colourful restaurants and bars.

Long and winding, the street breathed history, and it wasn't hard to picture the many kinds of people who'd travelled it in the past—Spanish conquistadors in shining armour, Indians in buckskin and feathers, Confederate militia in uniform.

Marigold was no map-maker, Tessa soon decided. It took her a while to find the shop required, and quite some time to choose from the extensive range of stock. Eventually selecting a sage-green cravat with a lozenge design, she added a matching handkerchief as her own contribution. Without any special request being made, her purchases were splendidly gift-wrapped. 'Our usual custom,' the owner smiled.

The florist's establishment turned out to be several blocks in a westerly direction so she paused at a pave-ment cafe en route and ordered fresh lime with soda and ice. The sun kissing her face as she sat sipping her drink, she mused on her good fortune. Mari was home, Ramon was happier, she and Tony had settled on to a steady course. Only one fly spoiled her New-World ointment—her sister's irascible doctor. But disapprove though she did of his temperament, Tessa had to admire Blair Lach-lan's dedication to his work, his single-mindedness.

Ambling leisurely, she made her way to 'The Flower Bower', a cool haven of blossom and fern. Selecting from sweet-smelling roses, carnations, orchids, gladioli, tiger lilies, chrysanthemums, she briefly envied the rich. How wonderful, to be able to surround oneself with flowers, the whole year through.

A melon-ball sun was sliding westwards by the time she arrived back at 'Los Arboles'. The front door was open and a delicious aroma of baking came wafting towards her. She sniffed appreciatively. Obviously, Wilma had been busy.

In confirmation, the maid came hurrying into the hall, wiping hands on apron. She looked flustered.

'Miss Tessa—I sure am glad to see you!' she burst out. 'Please, can you come and help me? It's Mrs Ruiz—I can't get her out of my kitchen! I know, and she knows, she should be resting, but there she is, hanging over my stove. So, the master's birthday's coming up, and she wants a cake, but why can't I be left to make it? Isn't my cooking good enough? She has only to say, and I'll pack my traps, find another situation!'

She shook her fist in the air. 'And this big party madam's planning tomorrow night, who's going to do all the work, that's what I'd like to know!'

Tight-lipped, arms akimbo, Tessa faced her sister. Pink-cheeked, pouting, Marigold sank on to a chromium-legged stool. Beside her on the table was spread the evidence of her labours—a flour-encrusted bowl, empty cartons, broken egg-shells, a pan of melted chocolate.

'Now Tessa, don't you start!' Guiltily, the miscreant stared up. 'An hour ago, I intended to be back in bed, and would've been, had I been allowed to get on, uninterrupted. You needn't look so cross—I've not been allowed to lift a finger, hardly; Wilma insisted she did all the fetching and carrying.'

'Then why not let her carry out the entire process?' Tessa snapped.

Marigold drooped. 'Well, it wouldn't have been the same, would it? I always do make Rae's birthday cake—a special gateau that's his favourite. Anyway, I was utterly bored with doing nothing—I'm pregnant, not stagnant! Surely a good husband deserves something personally prepared by his own wife, once a year?' Her voice had grown wheedling.

Tessa squared her shoulders. 'A good husband deserves a good wife—one who obeys her doctor's instructions. This very minute, you're going back to bed. Any more nonsense, and I'll catch the next plane back to England.'

'Now, what's all this about a party?' she demanded, as she straightened the top sheet. 'Are you out of your tiny mind?'

Marigold gave a little shrug, an appealing smile.

'No—it's just a tiny surprise I've planned for Rae—we always do have some kind of celebration. I rang around our friends, suggested they drop in for drinks, that's all. There's no need for anyone to start climbing up the wall—a caterer's supplying everything. All we have to do is enjoy ourselves. Me, I intend to recline on the day-bed looking soulful, like "La Dame aux Camelias".'

'Oh, yes? And look what happened to her!' Unconsidered, uncontrolled, the words rushed from Tessa's lips. Immediately, she could have bitten her tongue out. The reference to death, albeit oblique, had been stupid, cruel.

Letting out a loud wail, Marigold burst into tears.

'You don't care that I'm unhappy! You don't notice how depressed I am! You've no inkling what it's like to have every single nerve in your body on edge, to feel sick with anxiety . . .'

Filled with remorse, Tessa hurried to hug her sister.

'Oh, Mari, I'm sorry, I really am.' She kissed the damp cheek. 'The last thing I want is to upset you. But I am deeply concerned—we all are—to see that you don't over-tire, don't overdo things. All we want is to keep you well, keep you safe.'

'Oh, I know, I know,' Marigold gulped. Her golden curls tumbling round her face, she rested her head on her sister's shoulder. 'But—but—it's m-much better for me to have s-something to do, s-something to think about,' she sobbed. 'Please let the party go ahead, d-don't disappoint Rae. Remember, it's to ch-cheer him, as m-much as me. I promise f-faithfully not to lift a h-hand, not to d-do a thing. D-don't tell Rae—let's g-give him a surprise.' Her whole body heaved with emotion.

Tessa swallowed, blinked her eyes. 'Very well—but only if you give your solemn word that you'll do as you're told, in future. And you can start right now by handing over those cigarettes.'

Keeping her gaze fixed on her sister, Marigold had started to edge a cellophaned pack from under a magazine on her bedside table. As if it were a hot brick, she dropped it on to the bed-cover.

'B-bully!' she chided, but her blonde curls bobbed up and down. 'Okay, I'll do everything you say.' A sudden smile brightened her face. 'How about you getting on the phone to the gallery, getting hold of your Tony? Invite him over, tomorrow evening. I can't have you making all these sacrifices, just to look after little me. I can't have you becoming a nun!'

It was good seeing him again; though the separation had been only short, Tessa had missed him. The sight of his sturdy figure, his mane of raven hair, handsome face, set her heart fluttering. Quietly and discreetly Tony made himself indispensable, waited on Marigold, waited on everyone.

Dresden-shepherdess delicate in pale blue voile, the hostess reigned from her couch. True to her promise, she moved little, ate and drank sparingly, smoked not at all.

Though more numerous than Tessa had expected, the guests were not over-noisy, and they all behaved with the utmost consideration. The highlight of the evening was the arrival of Rosita, pushed in her wheelchair by her mother. Earlier in the day, Tessa had slipped over to their apartment, urged that they should both attend. Then, Rosita had raised every possible obstacle. These, in the meantime, she'd somehow managed to overcome, and she received a touching welcome. Watching Ramon's eyes mist with tears Tessa felt her throat tighten. Could this be the beginning of her friend 'coming-out'?

Making his formal speech of thanks following the cutting of the cake, Ramon flung his arms wide.

'My darling wife home, my dear sister and mother

visiting, my sweet sister-in-law over from UK, what more could I want?' He personified happiness; once again, he was the 'Laughing Cavalier'.

Throughout the reception corks popped, champagne flowed, food was proferred in abundance. By the time the last guests departed, it was almost midnight. Ramon's voice quavered as he expressed his gratitude.

'Tessa, angel, we simply couldn't do without you,' he said, kissing her on both cheeks. Gathering Marigold in his arms, he bore her off to their suite.

Tony slipped an arm round Tessa's waist. 'Ramon said it all—that same sentiment goes for me, too.' His lips touched her hair.

Smiling up at him, she slid from his hold.

'Work before play!' she instructed. 'First, we must see that everything's been cleared, then load the dishwasher. Wilma's dog tired.'

He worked with a will, but couldn't conceal his astonishment.

'All these glasses, all these dishes!' he exclaimed. 'Imagine owning all this lot! I'd hate to be lumbered this way—a few mugs and plates, that's all I need. Possessions turn people into prisoners.'

Tessa gave a tired nod. 'This time of the night, I'm with you all the way. When I marry, I'll go Chinese, I think—buy half a dozen small bowls and six pairs of chopsticks.'

His hand closed upon hers. 'You wish that we have four children?'

Her heart seemed to bounce. 'Of that question, I need notice, Mr Arretino. Watch out—you can't stop and make love, Wilma's still around.' Urgently, he was seeking her lips.

'The kitchen boy's worthy of his hire and demands his reward,' he murmured.'

'One kiss—then you must go,' she breathed.

'How cruel you are,' he whispered. 'You're such a tease. How is it that I can love you so much . . . ?'

In his arms, she forgot the world. Only when the

apartment door closed behind him did she come back to
reality. Collecting up the ashtrays in the big lounge,
switching off the lamps, she felt a stab of relief. The
party had passed off well, Ramon had been ecstatic,
Mari had been sensible, Rosita had plucked up her
courage and made a brief attendance. And she'd seen
Tony. All in all, Tessa was pleased.

All the same, she hoped and prayed that a certain
doctor didn't get to hear.

He strode in early next morning, swinging his black
medical bag. Immaculate in pearl-grey, he gave a sharp
glance round, lifted his head, sniffed like a blood-hound
on a scent.

'So, who's been smoking herself into ill-health?' he
demanded. 'Or have you been holding a cigar-makers'
convention?' The keen amber eyes flicked to the up-
ended trestle tables awaiting collection. 'Food and wine,
do I catch that aroma, as well?'

Pushing straight past Tessa, he shot into Marigold's
room. Unwarned, unsuspecting, the occupant was dancing her way to the bathroom, towards the cloud of steam
billowing through the connecting doorway. Hurrying to
keep pace with him, Tessa saw the whole scene. Dismay
flooded through her.

'What the hell . . . ? Marigold Ruiz, get back into
your bed, this instant!' Eyes glaring, arm thrust out,
finger pointing, he stood towering, Lincolnesque, lean,
formidable. Like a naughty child caught red-handed,
Marigold waddled sullenly back to her divan, belly
wobbling, buttocks indignantly weaving.

'Now, what's been going on, I'd like to know? Who
said you could get up, caper around? Didn't I give strict
orders about you resting? I guess it's as well I dropped
by, to check you over.'

He directed an impatient glance towards Tessa. 'For
Pete's sake, come in and shut the door! There's a remote
possibility I might welcome your help.'

Jittery with nerves, Tessa watched him carry out a

thorough examination, test heart and chest, measure arterial tension, press a finger into wrists and ankles. Except for the sound of heavy breathing, the room stayed silent, heavy with tension.

Straightening, he replaced stethoscope and sphygmomanometer in his case, clicked the lock.

'Well, that's it! You had your chance, Marigold, and well and truly have you blotted your copy-book! It's back to the clinic with you, at once. Square one, we've returned to—blood pressure up, signs of oedema . . .'

Marigold's mouth fell open. 'B-but I didn't do anything . . .' A big tear trembled her lashes, fell on to a flushed cheek.

Blair Lachlan raised a peremptory hand. 'Spare me the sob-stuff, my decision is final. When it comes to the safety of patients, I've a heart of stone. As for you, Miss Maitland, I'd like a word outside.'

With ill-concealed rage he confronted her, out in the hall. Looking timidly up, Tessa felt like a mouse, facing a lion.

'A waste of time, it'd be, enquiring into the whys, the wherefores,' he growled. 'Against my better judgment I yielded to your sister's pleas for a change of scene, and pressure from my staff for a respite! And, as I took care to inform you, the request wouldn't have been entertained, not for a minute, but for one circumstance— she was able to have the attention, full-time, of a trained nurse. That nurse was you, Miss Maitland, and I was under the impression I could trust a professional. Now I see all too clearly that I was mistaken.' The drawl had gone from his voice; his tone cut like a whiplash.

A few long strides, and he was at the outer door.

'I'll call Ramon from my office, advise him of my action. I want your sister back in the LS within the hour. Before midday, I plan to visit her there, in her room.'

His parting words he flung over his shoulder.

'I trust you realise the gravity of this situation? There could be a risk to both mother and child, if proper care isn't taken.'

Tessa's blood ran chill. Sick with despair, she stared after him. Her sister's life was in danger, and she was a total failure.

CHAPTER SEVEN

THE days that followed were more anxiety-making than
any Tessa had previously known. Not only was there
concern about Marigold's physical condition; her enforced return to the clinic took her to the brink of
hysteria. Sedated, she swung from a state of high excitement into abject apathy. If the first condition was
scaring, the second was pitiable. When eventually she
returned to somewhere approaching normal, even the
accompanying petulance was bearable.

Cause for concern undoubtedly continued. Tessa remarked an increased vigilance on the part of the staff,
more frequent tests and checks. Not blind to what was
going on, Marigold required constant reassurance,
Ramon also. Their help-mate had her work cut out.

In addition, she once again had to mount her guard
against Blair Lachlan. By using a service door at the side
of the LS building for her entrances and exits, she managed to reduce the hazard of running into him.

The narrowest escape she had was while she was with
Marigold, one afternoon. Nurse Fisher came bustling in
to announce the doctor was on his way to make an
unscheduled visit. Not daring to risk an encounter in the
corridor, Tessa dived into the bathroom, stood listening
against the closed door. Every move the doctor made,
every step he took in the adjoining bedroom, made her
catch her breath. What if he should want to wash his
hands, come bursting in, find her hiding? With a thumping heart she waited, wondering how it was the drawling
voice could charm, the personality repel? Relief overwhelmed her when she heard him depart.

As during her previous incarceration, Marigold's
friends rallied round in support and supplied a wide

variety of presents. One of these was a canary in a cage, the donor having heard Marigold frequently complain that she felt like an imprisoned bird.

'This little creature comes to cheer you with a trill,' the accompanying message read.

In theory, the idea was excellent, in practice, it didn't work. Not until someone with a sounder knowledge of the birds and the bees had added a mate of the opposite sex did singing commence. Thereafter the happy pair soloed and chorused the day long, from their wicker-basket house on the balcony.

Wistfully, Marigold watched their hoppings and flutterings.

'They're just like us, aren't they?' she said. 'Life without a partner lacks meaning. On one's own, what is there to sing about? Being on my tod in here has made me realise how very lucky I am, to have Rae.'

She sighed. 'I miss him most dreadfully, though he comes in each day. Without him, I feel only half a person. In every way, he's good for me; simply being with him gives me a happy glow. It's the sharing that matters, as much as the loving; fortunately, we like the same kind of things, the same sort of jokes. He can always make me laugh, and he never fails to give me confidence.'

'Mm-mm; that's just how it is with Tony and me.'

The blonde brows arched. 'It is? Rae and I have been wondering. You don't think you're seeing rather too much of our local artist, getting a shade too serious?'

Tessa tugged at her hair. 'No, I don't! What's bothering you?'

Marigold spread her hands. 'The differences . . . His background, for one; to say the least, it's unusual. Have you noticed that he never speaks of parents, brothers, sisters? More than once, I've tried to sound him out. All we do know is that he spent his early life in a primitive pueblo, and later went to a mission school, then on to art college.'

She patted a pillow into place. 'Don't get me wrong;

where he comes from doesn't matter all that much; it's just that—well, we think he's not good enough for you.'

Tessa tensed. All over again it was happening. This was Rosita's story. The pattern was repeating . . .

'Good enough? Tony's vastly more talented than me! Otherwise, Ramon wouldn't have taken him up, backed him with accommodation, money, equipment. He knows he's on to a sure thing, that Tony has a great future.'

Marigold bit her lip. 'Talented, yes; a great future, maybe . . . But that's not what we're bothered about.'

She raised questioning eyes. 'Our parents, have you thought about their reaction? They're both dears, but they do have their prejudices. What d'you think they'll say, if you present him as a future husband? About his ancestry, I mean.'

Tessa frowned. 'What's wrong with being part Italian? They love Italy . . .'

An impatient snort came from Marigold. 'That Arretino blood, it's got pretty diluted over the last century. More than anything, I'd say he's Navajo.'

Surprise rounded Tessa's eyes. 'You would?' Visualising the coal-black eyes, the broad build, the sallow skin, she stared. Of course, why hadn't she realised? But his Indian blood didn't matter to her, not in the slightest.

'So what? Isn't that something to be proud of? Everyone I've met says how fantastic a people they are.'

Vigorously, Marigold's curls swung from side to side.

'Tess, dear, it's not that easy! How to explain?' She rubbed her brow. 'The differences lie very deep, they'd be hard to overcome. Not everyone would accept him. Can't you hear dear Dad rolling out the old cliché, the one about "a touch of the tar-brush"? Okay, you and I don't think that way, nor do most folk of our age, but there are still people who do. When it comes to choosing a mate, the fewer disparities, the better.'

'Added to that,' she went on, 'it'll be quite a while

before Tony makes any money. If and when he does, he'll have a lot to spend out—debts to repay, a studio to establish, a lease to buy on an apartment. An artist's life is never very secure, never safe. And there are other things—his reluctance to conform to the world as it is, his opposition to progress. Why, Rae finds it hard to keep him to a regular work schedule, even. Believe me, it's not simply bias on our part—we have your interests at heart. We like him, we like him a lot, or Rae'd not have helped so liberally. Very easily, I can understand the attraction he has for you; he's kind, gentle, unusual. It's that very difference that makes us uneasy, the great ethnic gap. Let's face it, Tess, for an "Anglo" he's not a good match.'

Tessa knew a surge of fury. 'And what's so special about "Anglos"? About us? We're the daughters of shopkeepers, aren't we? As for his shade of skin, I've long been colour-blind. Living and working with hospital staff from all over the globe, I've learned that it's not the outer layers of a person that matter, but what's inside.' Her voice rose. 'I'm used to a cosmopolitan crowd.'

Marigold's eyes glinted. 'And we're not, is that what you're saying? Here, in Santa Fé—you must be joking! Let's put it simply—background is important, when it comes to settling down. The more similar two people are, the better the chance of success. Oil and water just don't mix.'

She sucked in her breath. 'The trouble is, you've been thrown together too much. All along, Rae's maintained you needed other distraction; he's been far from happy about you two getting close.'

'He's far from happy about Tony sparing the time to paint my portrait, that's what's irked him,' Tessa cried. 'As much as me, he has his precious Christmas show in mind! I'm fond of Tony, and I'll go on seeing him. So far as I'm concerned, he could come from the North Pole or Timbuctoo—anywhere! Anyway, why all this talk of marriage? As yet, it's not in my plans.'

Was she speaking the truth? She felt a blush crimson her cheek.

Marigold paled, ran twitching fingers over the top of her sheet, plucked at the hem.

'Oh, Tess, please—don't let's fall out! Quarrels I can't abide, not at present. I haven't the strength . . .' A tear splashed down. 'I want only what's best for you.'

Shame swept through Tessa. How could she be so lacking in feeling, so inconsiderate? What Mari said was true—she did always want the best, for herself, and for those she loved. Running to her, Tessa took her hand.

'Forgive me,' she whispered. 'I didn't mean to distress you—I should've had more sense. You mustn't get over-excited, you must stay calm.'

Marigold mopped her eyes. 'Now, don't start up like a mother-hen—I get enough fussing. Everytime I need to go to the loo, you'd think I'd lost both legs, the way "Fish" carries on. I feel so utterly useless. And Blair hasn't helped any. Today he warned I'm likely to have to stay here till junior arrives—till I'm confined, was the way he phrased it. What silly terms you doctors and nurses use—what am I now, I'd like to know? And "Fish" talks about my "lying-in". What's this, for mercy's sake?'

She sniffed audibly. 'Oh, well, if you can't beat 'em, join 'em, don't they say? Maybe they'll sign me on here as a recumbent aide. Mother used to get her patients rolling bandages in her VAD days, she said. What is the present day equivalent, I wonder, now that every hospital necessity comes ready wrapped, all snap, crackle, pop?' she sighed. 'This incarceration is a fate I'd not wish on my worst enemy.'

'Oh, come now,' Tessa chided. 'Count your blessings! A host of females'd be glad to be in your bed, have a baby on the way, a loving husband, a super home, fabulous friends. At least you can be miserable in comfort. Now, how about you doing something useful, compiling a list for the layette? If you don't, junior'll have to join the ranks of the naturists when he does arrive. Rosita, I happen to know, is plying her crochet-hook, but one woolly suit won't suffice. Here's your writing materials, get on with the job!'

She handed her sister a biro and a notepad.

'Talking of Ros, there's something I've been meaning to let you in on; with you being off colour, it slipped my mind. The day you started your brief trip home, I made a fascinating discovery. Remember my asking if you knew anything about her former beau, and you hadn't a notion? Well, I found someone who did—Dr Sep! And what do you know?—that man who travelled with me from Albuquerque, the scientist, I think he could be one and the same!'

Excitedly, she related the tallying details. Marigold listened, wide-eyed. 'Oh, how super, if you're right! Ros, if she can be made happy . . . A husband for her would be a godsend to Con and Sep, and to Rae. You'd better get going, get up to Los Alamos, and try to find that red-head—he was quite a looker!'

Full of hope Tessa set out, that bright October morning. The sky was the blue of a kingfisher's wing, the sun a great golden orb. It was a sightseeing bus she travelled in, on a circular tour. Bandelier Park it took in, the dwelling place of New Mexico's first settlers, proceeding on to Los Alamos, the eyrie of twentieth century scientists.

The Park was beautiful with its red sandstone cliffs, purple shadows, yellow cottonwoods, and the history of its cavemen enthralling, but Tessa found it hard to concentrate on all that the guide told them. Her mind was on Atomic City, and the man she hoped to find. Los Alamos, she wanted to get to Los Alamos.

On they travelled, over the majestic mountains. Suddenly, it was there, spread before them, a city of grid-iron squares and rectangles, straight roads, cubed housing; the rugged peaks, the curving plateau, the winding valleys, had been called to order by man.

While the other tourists went to view the museums of

science and history, Tessa set off on her own quest. From security point to enquiry office she was escorted, from official to official. Every single one was briskly polite and coolly efficient, but each in turn displayed a similar reaction to her enquiry. There was interest, then incredulity.

'You mean, you don't know the name of your— friend? You met him just that once?' The inevitable shrug, the spread of hands followed. 'Unless we're given a name, how can we identify him?'

In vain, Tessa listed the leads she had, repeated that she was seeking a scientist of around thirty, one who had red hair and a limp, who hailed from Boston, who'd arrived back at the establishment on a date in September. The response was non-committal.

'Write down your details, Ma'am, and we'll bear the matter in mind.'

Despondently, Tessa journeyed back to Santa Fé, spent the time in the bus reproaching herself. She'd been too hasty, too precipitate. A foreigner, a non US national, she'd gone snooping around a government establishment. Little wonder that she'd read suspicion in the eyes of the officers she'd met. Foolish, naïve, she must have appeared. Her cheeks burned.

Tony had been proved right, in his warnings. Hadn't he cautioned that she was taking too much on herself? Disappointed, disheartened, she longed for him.

He did his utmost, when they met, to console her. He betrayed no sign of smugness, didn't say 'I told you so!' But he did advise that she abandon her search.

'This trail you have is too random,' he said. 'And maybe you're not meant to turn hunter. This guy you call "Red", if Rosita still wants him that bad, won't she find him for herself, sooner or later? And if he's still keen, why hasn't he put in an appearance by now? Me, I'd have checked on what had happened to the family. Forget it, sweetie, give up; know when you're beaten.'

Marigold had the opposite view. With little else to occupy her mind, she accepted the tracing of 'Red' as a challenge, and was all for telephoning the airlines he'd travelled on, that day he'd met Tessa. They'd have records of passengers' names and addresses, she pointed out.

Meanwhile, she had acquired information that she was bursting to impart.

'Anna kept me company while you were gone; we had good "girl talk",' she said. 'She's been in SF a long time, knows all the dirt. Quite a bit she told me, about my doctor's past.'

Tessa pricked up her ears. 'Oh, yes? Like what?'

Marigold licked her lips. 'Like he had a fiancée, once. . . . Yes, I'd an idea you might be interested. The girl was one he met at college. A real beauty, she went on to become a model. Before he went overseas they were going steady and became engaged while he was in Vietnam. The day after he got back, she broke with him, took one look at the wounded hero and decamped. That was bad enough, but worse even was the note she left. In it she wrote that she couldn't live with a scarred man. Can you beat that, for cruelty?'

Tessa froze. Suddenly, she felt sick, sick in the pit of her stomach. Walking slowly to the window, she leant against it.

'How ghastly . . . !' she whispered.

'I'll say! I'm not surprised he got disillusioned. Some women! Can you understand anyone doing such a thing?'

Tessa shivered. 'No,' she said. But then, who was she to sit in judgment? It hadn't been her lot to suffer such a terrible shock, see someone she dearly loved return from war, injured. Clearly, she could picture the scene of that sad homecoming, visualise the air ambulance landing on the US drome, the stretcher cases being carried out, the walking wounded assisted. Among the waiting relatives and friends she saw a pretty girl, one whose life had revolved round beauty and glamour, one who'd had no experience of ugliness. How was she to know what wonders skilled surgery could work, that that livid scar would eventually heal, shrink to a long white line? Given patience, given time, all would have come good. Her heart ached for Blair Lachlan, but it also held sympathy for that girl.

Behind her, Marigold was still rattling on.

'And now, see what the rejection's led to—he's gone and landed himself with La Petersen! Maybe that lady has hidden charms—Anna suggests she could've restored his confidence, that being twice married, she knows a thing or two! Whatever the reason, it's all over bar the shouting—she's been in to inspect Rae's stock of engagement rings. Not that it brought him any trade— she'd the nerve to complain the selection wasn't good enough! How to win friends, and influence people—the wrong way! What was that, you mumbled?'

'Only that the remark was in character.' Tessa shrugged wearily. Nothing was going right, everything was going wrong. Out on the balcony the canary couple burst into song.

She wagged a finger at them. 'You don't know you're born!'

Rosita, too, announced that she had news, but first she wanted to know where Tessa had been hiding herself.

'I've missed you calling in,' she complained.

Tessa had no alternative but to tell of the trip she'd taken, expressed the view that Atomic City was a 'must' for every New Mexican visitor.

'Do you know the place?' A sudden impulse prompted the question. Closely, she watched her friend, and saw her shudder.

'Oh, yes . . . I used to play tennis there.' She glanced away.

An idea seized Tessa. If she could get her back up to Los Alamos, maybe she'd spot 'Red' or he'd spot her? Or she might get around to mentioning the name . . .

'The museums, have you visited those?' she asked. 'If I hired a suitable car, would you come? You could see the trees while they're red, and gold, and flame.'

'But that's what I am going to do, that's what I've been waiting to tell you,' Rosita exclaimed. 'Sep's at last arranged that picnic he's been on about, the pine-nut picking expedition; it's fixed for this coming Sunday. The church guild's providing the barbecue, everything. We're to be collected and driven into the hills in a maxi-bus.'

Her eyes shone. 'And I've a favour to ask—will you come along? Sep's stipulated that each disabled guest must have a fit escort to lend a hand with the pushing and lifting. It could be a bit much for mama, and she could use a leisure day. I'll have more confidence, if you're with me.'

Tessa didn't hesitate. 'Of course—I'll be delighted. There's just one thing—Sundays, I've a standing date with Tony. Would there be room in the bus for him as well, do you think? He'd be a great help.'

Rosita beamed. 'That'd be great—Sep mentioned he needed more able-bodied along. First check with him, and if he says yes, you can ask your boyfriend.'

The doctor agreeing, Tessa put the proposition at the next portrait sitting. Immediately, Tony said it would be his pleasure, that it was the duty of everyone to assist the less fortunate.

'Though the way the days are drawing in, Dr Sepulveda's only just getting this outing organised in time,' he said. 'The weather could soon be on the change.'

He looked longingly at her. 'Now, I pay more heed to the passing of time,' he said. 'Each day brings the end of your vacation that much nearer.' The gipsy eyes narrowed. 'Of course, it could be that you'll alter your mind and not go back to UK; choose to stay and look after Mari's kid.' Vigorously, he stirred a stick in the paint pot.

'There's nothing I'd like better,' Tessa admitted. 'But it's no go, I'm afraid. I'm a career girl, remember. I've to start my midder in January and that can't be delayed, without good reason.'

He faced her. 'Am I not sufficient reason? Tess, it's high time we had a talk, about the future. Jeepers, who's that outside? Okay, come in!'

A rap had rattled the sagging plank door; it opened to admit Ramon. He looked haggard and careworn.

'Ah, Tessa, I thought I might find you here,' he said. 'I was wondering if you'd care to eat out tonight—I'm bored stiff with snacking on my own. And there are things I'd like to talk over. "La Sevilla", would you like to try it? Swell! I'll come back and pick you up around eight. No, of course Mari'll not mind—she suggested the idea. I promised I'll look in on her early—soon as the gallery shuts.'

Brow creased, Tony watched him leave. 'Knew where you were all the time, didn't he? I've a notion he watches you come and go through his office window. This dinner date, I guess he cooked it up purposely. He used it as an excuse for dropping over, to see what we were doing.'

'I'm sure that's not so!' Tessa's protest was vehement. 'Rae's not like that; he'd not spy on me.'

'No, but on me he would!' Angrily, he threw down palette and brush, sent bright red paint splattering the wall. 'He thought something was going on in here, expected my hands to be occupied with you, and not my work! Mark my words, Tess, Rae doesn't approve of our friendship, and neither does your sister; it's on the cards that they'll aim to drive us apart.'

Pushing aside a pile of yellowing newspapers, he sank on to a bench. Tessa hurried to him, stroked his head.

'You mustn't be so suspicious,' she murmured. 'I know them better than you, and they're not mean-minded. You mustn't look on them as enemies; we owe them a lot. Without them I'd not have met you. They may not be cheering us on exactly, but they'd not act against us.'

He pulled her to him. 'You won't let them, will you? You won't let yourself be influenced against me?' His lips sought hers.

'I won't,' she promised, and savoured his kiss.

For the outing with her brother-in-law, Tessa put on her newest dress. Of lilac-blue silk jersey it had a plunging V-neck, a low-slung hip line. To complete the 'Gatsby-girl' look, she added a long string of pearls, fashioned a forehead kiss-curl, dusted her face with powder, pencilled a bow to her lips.

As intended, her appearance amused and cheered Ramon.

'You don't expect me to charleston, I trust?' he asked, giving his moustache a twirl. 'Don't let Mari see that get-up, or she'll be demanding one like it!'

Tessa giggled, 'For once, she'd have to wait. This dress is too straight up and down for an expectant mum! And I don't see Blair Lachlan allowing her out to shop.'

'Pregnancy, how it drags,' Ramon complained, as they drove to the restaurant. 'The months have never seemed so long. No-one thought to warn me what a strain it is, being a prospective father.'

She flashed him a teasing smile. 'You poor dear! Terrible, isn't it, the way men suffer? But don't have a fear—Maternity Sister was very reassuring, on this point; said she'd brought hundreds of babies into the world, and never lost a single dad!'

He laughed. 'You English, you have such a sense of humour!'

The restaurant was imposing. Candles flickered a welcome, roses centred the well-spaced tables, a soft melody floated from the shadowy depths.

'Wall-paper music only, I'm afraid,' Ramon said, as a waiter led them to a corner banquette. 'A pity, that. Tonight, I fancy I could foot the light fantastic, given the chance. I hope you'll enjoy this spot; locally, it's acquired a nickname. So many courting couples get engaged here it's become known as "The Hitching Post". Because it tends to get pretty full, I phoned ahead to order the house speciality.'

He ordered wine, then took her hand. 'It's fun, getting out for an evening once again. Usually, Mari and I dine out two or three times each week, but it's no fun on one's own. May I say how sweet you look, in that twenties garb?'

Lifting her hand to his lips, he planted a kiss square on her palm. His beard tickled her skin and she let out a little scream. Several faces turned in their direction.

He waved a hand at her in mock reproof. 'That's no way to react to an old Spanish custom! We Latins know a thing or two, when it comes to kissing; we don't neglect a woman's tenderest spots!'

He winked. 'You should find a true man, Tessa, one with conquistador blood in his veins. That way, you'll experience the full meaning of love.'

She raised her brows. 'You believe the Latins have a monopoly there? My limited experience doesn't lead me to entirely agree with you.'

Their eyes met, and she saw the twinkle fade, his face settle into serious lines.

'I joke, of course. But do take care, dear sister-in-law, when it comes to plighting your troth. Trust the familiar rather than the strange; the known, rather than the unknown. Foreign products can carry more glamour than the home-produced; from cars to cameras, clothes to furnishings, that holds true. And it applies to men also. Temporarily, the exotic can outclass the conventional, lead to danger.'

Tessa straightened. Here it comes, she thought; Tony was right. The warpaint's on, the tomahawk's coming out! She ran nervous fingers along the table edge. To her great relief, the arrival of one waiter with wine, another with the hors d'oeuvres trolley, interrupted the conversation.

But Ramon was not to be put off course.

'Tony, exactly what is he up to these days?' he asked, spearing an olive. 'Why so much playing hookey? I get kind of tired finding that dog-eared note pinned to his studio door, "Back in half an hour". A senseless message, if ever there was one. Who's to know when the recess started, when it'll end? And where does he get to?'

Tessa shrugged. 'Not far, that's for sure. Occasion-ally, he slips over to the plaza, sketches the trees there when he requires a background. Anyway, he needs to take the air sometimes. It's not good for anyone to be cooped up indoors all day, especially an artist; lack of oxygen dulls the brain.'

She waited a moment before she spoke again, waited until Ramon had swallowed a copious draught of cold white wine.

'Is it quite fair, suspecting that he tries to skip work?' she enquired gently. 'He's always hard at it, whenever I call.'

Ramon rolled his eyes. 'Once a week, twice at the most, you're there; there are other days, other times. For you, he's bound to be ready and waiting.'

The approach of a laden trolley made him tap the rim of her plate.

'Eat up, here comes our Paella Valenciana—I hope it'll be to your taste.'

The dish took a while in serving. By the time their plates were piled with saffron rice, golden chicken, silvery mussels, pink clams, and garnished with ar-tichoke hearts, chorizo, green peppers, Tessa had thought of a way to veer the talk: better a change than a controversy, she'd decided.

'Your turquoise cuff-links, they're Navajo, aren't they?' she asked. 'How is that kind of jewellery made? Where did it originate?' It was, she well knew, one of his favourite lines in the craft shop. Immediately, he was away, enthusiastically launched on a description.

'The Spaniards learnt it from the Moors, then brought the skill from the old world to the new,' he informed her. 'They taught it to the Mexicans, who passed it on to the Indians.'

He went on to tell how Navajo shepherds fashioned the silver wire settings while tending their sheep. Once embarked on talk of business, there was no holding him. His plans, his hopes, his commitments, his worries, he revealed. Realising his need of a sounding-board, Tessa listened attentively. Her parents being shopkeepers, she'd imbibed an interest in trade along with her mother's milk, had been acquainted with the intricacies of buying and selling since she was counter-high. The comments she made, the suggestions she tentatively put forward, received approving nods from Ramon.

'You're a great girl, Tess,' he said, patting her hand. 'A great consolation. Right now, Mari and I couldn't manage without you. All the time, you give of your best.'

She spread her hands. 'Precious little, I do, actually —it's just that I make it look a lot. And, but for you, don't forget, I'd not be here in Santa Fé, enjoying all the beauty, all the luxury; intead, I'd be toiling away in a busy ward.'

She played with a spoon. 'My one regret is that I can't help more. But do go on—tell me all that's on your mind. Rest your troubled head on Auntie Tessa's shoulder, if that'll help!'

Chuckling, he made a pretence of doing so, rubbed his beard against her cheek.

'Careful, Tess! Too much wine and sympathy, it could be bad, even for the most besotted husband!'

He kissed her hand. 'I've not enjoyed a meal so much since Mari was whisked into the LS; before that even, pregnancy was playing havoc with both our appetites. Now, what for dessert? The chocolate mousse they serve here's an experience, or maybe you'd prefer a lemon sherbet?—sorbet, your side of the Atlantic. Waiter, two sherberts, and bring a selection of liqueurs with the coffee.'

Oblivious of time they sat chatting, forgetful of surroundings. Not until the bill was presented did Tessa take a look round the big room.

It had grown late and the place was emptying. Observing a mezzanine gallery along the opposite wall, she decided it would be the best place to sit, to get a full view of the restaurant.

Her gaze travelled on, then darted back. That ash-blonde hair, that exceptional height—Debra Petersen, Blair Lachlan! How small Santa Fé was.

The couple had risen and were preparing to leave. She watched the doctor drape a cloak round the willowy shoulders, the secretary smile fondly up, and felt her stomach turn over. In that split second she saw the pair as lovers, and the thought wasn't pleasing. Had Debra found an engagement ring to her liking? Was the marriage merely a matter of dotting 'i's', crossing 't's'?

As if sensing a watcher, the elegant blonde sharply turned her head, and her eyes met Tessa's. Baring her white teeth in a stagey smile, she linked a proprietorial arm through Blair Lachlan's. Giving the semblance of a bow, he led her out.

The bill paid, Ramon stood waiting.

'Was that a shiver I saw?' he asked. 'You're tired, I've kept you up, wearied you with my talk. Thank you for sparing me your time, being such a patient listener. These days, I'm not too clever managing on my own, marriage to Marigold has spoiled me for going solo.'

They reached the parking lot as the red Porsche pulled out. Ramon jerked a thumb.

'Third time lucky, I trust. Who Petersen's husband was, I don't know, or anything about her first husband either, but she sure gets through her men at a fair lick. Here's wishing Blair better luck—he's a great guy.'

He reverted to talk of business and spoke of nothing else the entire journey home. Absently, Tessa nodded or shook her head at what seemed appropriate moments. Her thoughts remained on the intimate scene she'd just witnessed.

Why Debra Petersen? To her, the secretary looked as synthetic as her hair. She hated the way those green eyes appraised her clothes every time she ran into the woman, shot up like tabs on a cash register. Lacking warmth, lacking an interest in people, she didn't appear a suitable wife for a medical man, and certainly not for Blair Lachlan.

CHAPTER EIGHT

It simply didn't occur to Tessa to be on her guard as she went into the apartment block. At the LS yes; there, she never neglected to keep a watchful eye, but on her home ground at 'Los Arboles' there seemed no need for vigilance.

Her mind was on Marigold. That morning, her sister had been more than usually peevish, annoyed by the airlines refusing to divulge any information concerning their auburn-haired passenger. Wondering how to cheer her, Tessa was halfway to the elevator before the approaching tall figure impinged on her consciousness.

Her first reaction was one of alarm, the second one of relief. Blair Lachlan wasn't looking in her direction. His amber eyes fixed on the exit, he was striding straight towards it, a preoccupied expression on his lean face.

Remarkably fit and handsome he looked, his suit of cavalry twill immaculately cut, skin glowing brown against the cream silk of his shirt, tawny curls bouncing as he walked.

Heart bounding, she stepped to the side of a potted palm, froze on the spot, like a rabbit spying a fox. If she kept still, she mightn't be observed. Right past her he strode, and she drew breath, but the respite was brief. A few long steps and he suddenly slowed, swivelled round.

'Why—hello there! I almost missed noticing . . . Last evening, you had a good time?' He hooded his eyes. 'How come we don't meet up these days, at the clinic? Your—other interests, they don't permit you to spend as much time there?'

She gaped. Despite the note of sarcasm it held, the husky drawl had set her pulse racing. This incredible man, how could he manage such a calm approach? Their last meeting, the way he'd enticed her into his home, his rapacious groping, could he have forgotten? One final fling, had it been, before committing himself to La Petersen?

He stood measuring her, taking in every saddle-stitch of her Bokhara-red jacket.

'I visit most days still.' She managed to steady her voice. 'Mari seems better—you're pleased with her progress?'

He tilted his head. 'Mm-mmm. With luck, I hope to get her to full term. If necessary, we'll induce, but that's something I prefer not to do, unless essential. This stay, she does seem to have settled in better, after a poor start.'

He gave a hitch to the medical bag in his hand.

'We had a sick call here on third, so I looked in on Rosita as I was in the block—Sep's suggestion. Very chirpy she seemed, full of chat about the pinon picnic that's being planned.' He raised one brow. 'You see her often?'

'Frequently. She's become a very good friend.'

The grin he gave was slanting, attractive. 'Exactly the description she gave of you. You're doing a great job, there.'

Tessa felt her cheeks glow. How could he stand there in that calm, detached manner? Beneath his scrutiny, in such close proximity, she was uneasy; urgently, she wanted to get away. But she musn't waste this opportunity. She moistened her lips.

'Rosita's chance of walking again, how would you rate it?'

'Hmm.' He stroked his scarred cheek. 'I'm not her medic or a specialist, it's not for me to say. The disturbance of function appears to have no physical cause. It could originate up here.' He tapped his head. 'The mind can greatly influence the body.'

He shrugged. 'In such a case, who can tell? The top men have all been baffled. Medicine's still far from having all the answers.' He coughed. 'Touching on the professional, I've something to ask you, a favour. A group of us medics help to man free clinics, at regular intervals, donate a little of our time. On occasion, I have need . . . Hell, that doorman, he's beckoning this way— I guess he wants me to move my car. The forecourt was full when I arrived—I had to double-bank. Another day . . .'

He went racing off, long legs speeding over the marble tiles.

Puzzled, Tessa turned towards the elevator. What had he been going to say, to request? She should be so lucky that he'd ask anything from her, as a nurse, after what had happened with Mari! What could he have in mind? Thankful that their meeting had passed off with so little embarrassment, she gave a sigh of relief.

On the face of it, the task appeared simple. Deputed by Marigold to shop for her baby's layette and provided by her with a list, Tessa set off lightheartedly. Before very long she experienced difficulties. Seeking a specialist mother-and-baby store, she failed to locate the one suggested. Trying successive boutiques, she met with perplexed stares; bewildered assistants passed busily on to the next customer in line. Several such rebuffals eventually caused her to groan, tug despairingly at her hair.

'Can I be of any help, do you think?'

The question, voiced in a transatlantic tone, came from behind. Glancing back, Tessa saw a slender woman in her middle years neatly dressed in navy blue, her silvering hair smartly cut urchin style.

'Maybe if I took a look at that memo?' She held out a slin hand. 'Ah, yes, I think I detect your problem— whoever made this out is another Brit, I guess; there's a difference in terminology. For napkins read diapers, though mothers these days mostly use the disposable kind—'Pampers'. Vests, they're undershirts, over here, and we call a face-flannel a wash-cloth. Regarding the sundries, cotton-wool's known as absorbent, and you should ask for nipples, not teats, with the feeding-bottles. A baby's dummy, that's a pacifier this side, remember, if one should be needed. Now, let me advise you where to buy what you want.'

Two bright blue eyes surveyed the list. 'You need a dry-goods store for the drapery items; a druggist, for the others. And for catalogues of cots and prams, go to "Cribs and Carriages" in the Mall.'

She smiled graciously as Tessa thanked her. 'The British and the Americans are one people divided by a common language, didn't someone say—GBS, was it? You look like you could do with some refreshment, and I was just planning to get a coffee. Next door, there's a drug store; care to join me?'

'My, but it's good to hear a true blue British accent,' she went on, when they were seated on high stools at a spotless counter. 'This baby shopping, it can't be for you?' The shrewd gaze slid from Tessa's slim waist to her ringless left hand.

'No—it's for my sister.' Tessa gave brief details. 'It's her first child she's expecting, and now she can't get to the shops.'

'Marigold Ruiz? She is your sister?' The fine brows arched. 'I know her by sight—she's often at the opera, with her husband. She's so fair, and he's so dark, they make a striking couple. My son is well acquainted—he's their medic. Come to think of it, I recall him mentioning he'd admitted your sister to the LS. It was my late husband who founded it. I'm Lenore Lachlan.'

Blair's mother! Tessa's mouth went dry. Had Mrs Lachlan recognised her? Did she know her for the girl she'd seen sprawled on her son's knee, that night? One nervous glance and she knew a certain reassurance. Her new acquaintance showed no sign of having seen her before, and Tessa remembered that the lighting in the 'Los Pinos' lounge had been mercifully dim. How odd that she should bump into the mother so soon after encountering the son. Inwardly, she felt an agitated flutter.

'I—I'm T-Tessa Maitland,' she said, catching her breath.

'You're here on holiday? Have just arrived?'

Tessa gave a quick nod, one of relief. 'Yes, only recently.'

Mrs Lachlan directed her gaze full upon her. 'Never would I have guessed—that you and Mrs Ruiz are sisters, I mean. How long shall you be staying? Three months?—that's splendid! And what do you do with yourself, back in dear old England?'

Approvingly, she nodded, on learning.

'Nurse, meet an ex-nurse! Edinburgh Royal, I trained. Blair's dad was a US Army doctor; we met up at a hospital dance. Have you heard of GI brides, ever? Well, I was one, and our son was a honeymoon baby. '46, that was; an age ago, though the years have simply flown.'

Thoughtful, she stirred the froth on her cup of espresso, as if seeing the disappearing whirls as vanished years.

'Strange, isn't it, how a chance meeting can change one's entire life? Before World War Two I'd not set eyes on a single American except on the cinema screen; where I come from, they were as rare as Hottentots. Who'd have guessed, then, that I'd end up here in lovely Santa Fé, half-way across the world?'

She gave a lift of her shoulders. 'Ah, well, I've no regrets save one—that my dear Robert didn't live to enjoy a well-earned retirement, and that we had but the one child.'

A sigh escaped her lips. 'Life can be hard on an "only". Young, they can feel solitary; adult, they get burdened with the sole responsibility of ageing parents. Sometimes I wonder I've not been in part to blame for Blair dragging his feet over marrying. Of course, he did have one ghastly let down, and then there was the challenge of getting the clinic back on its feet. Losing faith in women, he sought refuge in his work, became wed to it—too much so, in my opinion.'

She fluttered a hand. 'But very soon, he should get a chance to tail off a little, get more free time—they're getting an extra medic in, to assist. Marriage could become a possibility, but I do hope he won't go and settle for whatever's nearest to hand . . .'

The blue eyes clouded. Debra Petersen, was she thinking of Debra Petersen? Who else . . . ? Tessa gulped a mouthful of her drink.

Fishing in her handbag, Mrs Lachlan produced a visiting card.

'Here's where I live,' she said, passing it over. 'You may find yourself in need of a guide again, while your sister's sick. Any time I can be of assistance, please do call me, and if you find yourself near my home, drop in. You know the district? Have a good stay, and have a good day.'

She departed, leaving Tessa with an inner glow, a feeling that she'd found a friend. A pity that the son lacked his mother's easy manner, her approachability.

The shopping rendered straightforward, it was speedily completed. Arms piled with packages, Tessa made her way across the plaza. The warm sun shone bright on the central obelisk, glinted on the ear-rings of a squatting hippie, turned to fiery copper the hair of the thin man striding the path way ahead.

Tessa looked, blinked, caught her breath. 'Red', it was 'Red', Rosita's boyfriend, the man for whom she'd been hunting!

'Hi!' she cried, 'Wait! Please wait!' Hoping he'd heard, expecting him to turn, she threw up a hand, waved vigorously. But the man didn't look back. Deaf to her summons, he marched straight on. Unbalanced by the movement of her arms, the parcels cascaded down. Stooping to pick them up, she caught the clasp of her bag in a loop of string. Flying open, it released the contents. Money, keys, cosmetics, went shooting over the ground.

Tessa's immediate instinct was to temporarily abandon the lot and give chase, return to retrieve when capture had been made. One quick glance round, and she changed her mind. Hungry-eyed, the hippie had risen to his feet, was avidly regarding the rolling dimes, the escaping dollar bills. Feverishly, she scraped the scattered possessions together, thrust them back. Arming her packages, she resumed her pursuit. Long distanced, her quarry was crossing the road.

'Hi!' she called again, but her shout was lost in the traffic noise. Launching herself into the lines of moving cars, she threaded between bonnets and boots at a breakneck speed. Horns honked, drivers bellowed uncomplimentary remarks, but on she ran.

Panting, she reached the pavement, craned her neck to peer above the gaggles of lunch-time amblers. Where had he gone? In the nick of time, she caught a glimpse of the red halo vanishing into a side-street.

Her heart lurched. Could she possibly catch him up? So much, so very much, depended on it. Sweat dampening her brow, she weaved an erratic path between the loitering pedestrians.

The corner rounded, she could have screamed her relief. Neck bent, there he was, studying the menu outside a café. Renewing her grip on her burdensome parcels, she went lumbering up.

'Re—mem-ber me?' she gasped out. 'Al—bu—querque, the plane . . .'

Her words trailed for the man had turned. The hair, that was the same, though here there were silver threads, and the face was freckled, but the lines were deeply etched. His clothes gave further proof, if any were required, that she'd made a mistake, for the collar he wore was stiff, white, circular, and his shirt was black.

Open-mouthed, round-eyed, Tessa stared at the priest.

'I—I'm s-sorry,' she blurted out. 'I thought you were someone I knew . . . you look very like him.'

The priest gave her a kindly smile. 'I'm sorry, too. If your friend closely resembles me he has my sympathy.'

'Oh, no, I see now . . .' Tessa's confusion grew. 'It's your colouring, your build . . .' Inexplicably, she heard

herself add, 'You—you don't have a younger brother,
by any chance?'

Beatifically, the priest spread lily-white hands. 'All
men are my brothers. But by blood, I'm afraid I was my
mother's only son.' A twinkle lit his eyes. 'You seem
somewhat overloaded, my dear. Can I help, at all?'

'Thank you, but no—I think I'll take a little rest, have
a cold drink.' Tumbling the parcels on to a forecourt
table, she collapsed on to a chair.

Watching him walk away, she felt furious with herself.
How blind could she get? Why hadn't she stopped to
take a closer look, to think properly? The priest had an
even step, walked without the hint of a limp! Tony had
been right, she should give up. The search for 'Red' was
becoming an obsession.

Marigold was highly amused when she heard the story.

'Go on like that and you'll have the police on your
trail; they'll suspect you're a tramp,' she warned. 'Over
here that, remember, means prostitute, so you'd better
watch out.'

She wiped the tears of laughter from her eyes. 'Imagine you, chasing a man of God! Now, may I see what
you bought for my child?'

Occupied in an inspection of the purchases, she didn't
heed her sister's long face, the monosyllabic replies she
gave to her questions. Disappointed, disenchanted,
Tessa made an early departure, directed her steps to
Tony's studio. The fruitless quest had left her shaken,
left her in need of consolation.

The grubby square of card hit her eye as she turned
into the cobbled yard. Even before she drew sufficiently
near the door to read the words, she knew the message it
bore: 'BACK IN HALF AN HOUR.'

Her heart plummeted. Where was he? When she most
longed for him, he was missing.

She glanced at her watch. A late snack lunch, that's
what he'd be having; he'd not be long.

The studio door opened at a touch, and she wasn't

surprised. As she was aware, he seldom bothered to lock.

'What do I own that anyone would wish to steal?' he'd asked, when she'd commented on what to her seemed carelessness. 'Some paint, canvas, a few brushes, a quantity of frames—things that'd only interest another painter, and artists don't thieve one from the other. My clothes, they'd not be worth taking.'

For a while she rested on the model's throne, the only available seat. Uneasy, restless, she soon rose, started to meander around between tables littered with cans, papers, bundles of rag, bottles of turpentine and linseed oil, pick her way over a floor cluttered with crates, lengths of board. Higgledy-piggledy, the equipment lay scattered. Everything had a coating of dust and cobwebs draped the windows.

Even in Tony's dynamic presence the general neglect had been apparent; in his absence it hit forcibly. Wandering through the partition door, she sneaked a glance into his 'pad' at the back, saw blankets jumbled on a bunk, a rough rope slung across one corner which acted as wardrobe and carried creased shirts and slacks. Separated by a wall of wooden boxes, the living area housed a battered table, chairs, a shallow sink, a rusting 'fridge, an ancient stove, shelves holding dented pans and a line of canned foods.

She stood aghast. What a way to live! Her heart ached for Tony. Desperately, he needed someone to look after him. How could he live, let alone work, in such a tip? This muddle must surely slow him down. Properly organised, he'd be able to step up production, keep in Ramon's good books, get well known, make some real money. She'd suggest a general tidying.

She glanced at her watch. Twenty minutes had gone by, twenty wasted minutes. Why wait, lose more time? Why not tackle the job, that very instant?

Knotting her scarf round her head to protect her hair, fastening a large piece of rag round her waist to act as apron, she set to work. Sorting like with like, grading according to type and size, she made a great clearance. A mangy broom and a buckled shovel coming to light, she swept the plank floor, then proceeded to take a damp cloth to the grimy windows.

Standing back to survey the results of her labours, she glowed with satisfaction. Rough and ready though the cleaning had been, it was better than no cleaning at all. Anxious to surprise Tony, to please him, she'd carried out the work as if her life depended on it, not wasting a second. Next time, she'd do a more thorough job.

She checked her watch. A whole hour had elapsed, sped by. Tony surely couldn't be much longer?

'Oh, come on, do!' she begged aloud, eager to witness his delight. As if in answer, pattering feet sounded on the cobbles in the yard. Whipping off kerchief and apron, she stood expectant, her heart thumping in her breast.

Whistling softly, he came in, the tune coming in little snatches. Abruptly, it died, as his steps slowed.

'Tessa? You? Here? It's not your usual day . . .'

Amazement rounding his gipsy-eyes, he swivelled his head. 'What the deuce . . . What's been going on? You've never—dusted . . . ?'

'Oh, yes, I have!' Beaming with pride, she waved the cloth in her hand. 'Dusted *and* cleaned. As yet, it's not new-pin bright, but next going over, it'll be much better. And now there's a place for everything, and everything's in its place. Now, you won't have to waste precious time hunting for what you require. See, the paints are over here, the brushes next to them . . .'

An iron hand gripped her arm; she stopped mid-flow. Anticipating a grateful hug, a rewarding kiss, she tilted her head, looked up.

She saw the chiselled lips tighten, heard him catch his breath.

'Oh, no!' he groaned, clapping his hands to his face. 'How could you? You, you've got to be crazy! After all these weeks of visiting, haven't you learnt? The painter's worst enemy, you've gone and stirred to life! Dust, it sticks to oils—the paint can take weeks to dry! Why do you think I spread things out, the way I did? No-one, but no-one, is allowed to touch my studio! All those canvases you've stacked, you've likely ruined!'

The quarrel was sharp, intense. Upset, bitterly disappointed, Tessa wept tears of remorse. His anger vented, Tony took her in his arms, mopped her cheeks, murmured soothingly. 'You didn't understand, weren't to blame,' he assured her. 'Forgive me blowing my top. I was on edge—about work, about you, about everything. This courting business, it sure is a strain, plays havoc with my nerves. It's like—it's like trying to drive a horse team with one hand on the rein, the other on the whip! Of course, you didn't realise . . .'

He kissed the tip of her nose. 'Let's take a close look at the canvases, see exactly what has happened.'

A careful examination made, he had to admit he'd been unduly alarmed, that there was nothing that a touching up here, a small re-painting there, couldn't put right. The portrait about which he showed most concern, one he didn't permit her to see, had never allowed her to view, was Tessa's own picture. Stood face to the wall, it hadn't suffered damage, he said.

Surveying the tidied room, he ran his fingers through his hair.

'The problem's going to be locating what I want,' he said. 'Okay, so it was chaos before, but it was organised chaos, I knew where to put my hand on everything. This, sweetie, is a studio, not a sterile unit! That's the trouble these days—everyone's on the tidy-up kick. Folk, even, get tidied away into institutions. It's the kind of world I don't care for, much. Where I come from they may have only earth johns and mud floors, but they don't lack humanity; pueblo people act for the common good.'

He took her hand, stroked her fingers. 'Come on, let's declare a recess, go get ourselves a cool drink.'

Dear, sweet, kind Tony, Tessa reflected, when she left him. He'd had every reason to feel seriously riled, every cause to be cross. Thoughtlessly, rashly, she'd acted, but his rage had rapidly died, and he'd been full of contrition. He knew how to say he was sorry, he was big, generous-hearted enough. Full of plans for the pinon picking outing, they'd parted, close friends again, both of them eager to see Rosita's reaction on getting up into the mountains.

Faithfully, Tony had promised to be on time, but the coach had to wait a full ten minutes for him to arrive. As if the day had no ending, he sauntered up to the assembly point with a sketch pad tucked under his arm, and only with effort did Tessa bite back the reproof her lips had framed. Soon, she was glad to have done so, for he proved an invaluable aide. Up and down the bus he wandered, pointed out places of interest they were passing to the disabled passengers, chatted sympathetically.

Seated beside the driver, Dr Sepulveda kept a watchful eye on the contingent.

'We've a heart case along, and a paraplegic,' he confided to Tessa. 'One can't be too careful.'

Starting low, in whispers almost, the conversation gradually swelled to a persistent hum. Eyes grew bright, voices high-pitched with excitement. For people used to existing between four walls, seeing life second-hand through TV, the sight of the open country, the vivid colours of autumn, proved a breathtaking thrill.

Cheeks tinged the shade of her shocking-pink dress, Rosita gazed in wonder about her.

'What a lot I've been missing!' she murmured. 'It's strange, but I don't feel the least bit scared, though it's been ages since I was out. In a car, I think I'd have been frightened, but with all this company and Sep here to look after everyone, I'm loving every second.'

Tessa's eyes pricked with unshed tears. Fervently, she hoped that the day would bring a break-through for her friend, a new beginning.

The foothills reached, the coach drew into a designated picnic area equipped with stone benches and tables, a barbecue pit, garbage baskets, toilets. Before climbing out, Lazaro Sepulveda made use of the dash-board radio link to report their location back to the clinic.

'A precaution, in case I'm wanted,' he explained. 'Blair and I, we usually try to maintain contact. With our new assistant now arrived, I'm hoping we'll be getting ourselves a little more free time.'

Under his capable direction, the disabled members of the party were assisted out and established beneath the trees, the provisions unloaded, the barbecue ashes raked to life, fir cones and logs piled on. Very soon the air was scented with pine intermingled with the aroma of sizzling steak and bacon. Coke and lemonade, beer and wine were poured; the atmosphere became heady with pleasure. So much joy derived from such a simple out-ing: Tessa felt deeply moved. Looking round at the smiling faces, she knew an increased respect for the little doctor. Thoughtfully, imaginatively, he'd organised the trip.

Luncheon over, the remnants of food were scattered to the birds. The equipment repacked and reloaded, the rubbish gathered, some of the picnickers elected to take a nap, others went off to search for pine-nuts.

Initially, Rosita chose to remain in the clearing, and Tessa stayed with her. Unable to doze, she grew restive.

'That brilliant sky!' Rosita peered up through the branches. 'I'd love to get higher, get a wider view. Could you manage to push me in my chair, do you think? It would be thrilling to look out over the valley, try to spot our old home. Your Tony, would he come and help?'

Leaping to her feet, Tessa glanced across to where he sat sketching.

'He's busy drawing pictures, mementoes for people to take back,' she observed. 'We'll not bother him. Don't worry, I can easily manage.'

At first the track they followed was smooth, well-worn. When it narrowed, became stony, Tessa took a more winding but less difficult route through the trees. It led to the edge of a steep bluff, to a path that seemed to soar into the sky, into a world of limitless blue. Below, lay a deep canyon lined with trees, beyond ridge upon ridge of high peaks. Rosita drew in great gulps of fresh air.

'It's magical,' she whispered. 'Look at the trees all red and gold—they look dressed ready for carnival! Leave me here, give me time to drink it all in, and you go on; climb as high as you want, collect sufficient pine-nuts for us both, fill these plastic bags I brought along.'

Selecting a level surface, Tessa firmly wedged the wheelchair between two large rocks, clicked on the brake.

'You'll be all right? You're sure?' she asked. 'You won't be lonely? Won't get bored?' The pushing had been hard going, and she was glad to have a rest.

Rosita shook her dark curls. 'Bored, with the world at my feet—you must be joking!' She waved a hand. 'Off you go; good hunting.'

On and up Tessa wound her way, taking little glances back until her friend was lost from sight. A gentle breeze ruffled her hair, and the sun warmed her cheeks; she felt at peace. Once again, there was the pellucid dazzling light; once again, she experienced a sensation of weightlessness, seemed not to walk but to float. From blue-green pine to blue-green pine she moved as if in a dream and collected up chocolate brown nuts, the spillings from petalled cones. The plastic bags filled, she started on the downward trek. Approaching the promontory where she'd left Rosita, she watched for sight of her friend round every bend. With the suddenness of lightning, the glint of chromium shone through the trees, and she excitedly held up her gleanings.

'Ros! I've collected all these!' she called. 'And there are tons more nuts, there for the collecting . . .'

Her words died. The chair was there, exactly as she'd wedged it, but the seat—the seat was empty!

Her heart stood still, then started to race madly, to bang in her ears. Rosita, she couldn't have moved, not unaided! Hurrying over to the chair, she passed trembling hands over the back seat, unable to credit what she saw.

'Rosita!' she cried, 'Ros, where are you?' The call quavered to an end as her gaze fell to the bluff's jagged edge. Could she—had she—was it possible? Had she leant forward, over-balanced, gone hurtling down? Please God, not that! For a moment she froze, then urged herself to creep cautiously forward, peer over the edge, down into the chasm. Relief surged through her as she detected no branches broken, no foliage disturbed, no rocks dislodged. But where . . . ?

Spinning round, she searched the shadows beneath the trees, spied a line of vivid pink close to the ground.

'Ros, oh, Ros!' she cried, racing to the prone body. 'How—Why?'

Plunging to her knees, she touched the dark head, and her fingers came away sticky, damp, bright crimson. Blood! Freely, it was flowing, from a deep cut.

Rosita stirred slightly, gave a low groan. 'Te-ss? . . . that you?' Her voice was indistinct. 'The sky—it drew me—had to try my legs . . . fell on something hard. My head . . .'

Words trailing, head sagging, she went limp, slipped from consciousness.

'Ros, Ros, please don't pass out!' Agonised, the cry burst from Tessa's lips. This was all she needed. Her friend lay injured, comatose. How to get her back into her chair, down the mountainside? How to lift the plump body? Was it safe to move her?

Briefly, Tessa experienced panic. In hospital, she could have coped without thinking. With skilled help on hand, a specified procedure, she'd have known the routine. But here, on a steep slope . . .

A few muddled seconds, and her training surfaced, came to her rescue. 'First, treat any haemorrhage.' As if in print before her on a textbook page, the instruction came stark and clear. Folding a clean handkerchief taken from her pocket, she bound it over the wound, using the sash of her dress to tie it in place.

Help, she must immediately summon help. Dr Sep, he was the man to get. Leaping up, she filled her lungs with air, then bellowed with all the strength she could muster:

'Dr Sepulveda, help! Help, we need help!'

The light breeze scattered a few drying leaves. High, high above, a miniscule plane droned across the sky, trailed vapour in a white line; a buzzard hovered on spread brown wings. Otherwise, no sound, no movement.

Louder, more desperately, she yelled, then again. If nobody heard the appeal, came to their aid, she'd have to leave Rosita as she lay and rush down to seek aid.

From far below, she caught the faint murmur of voices. The picnickers couldn't be far away; hope sprang up within her.

Crunch, crunch, crunch. Scarcely audible at first, the sound grew in strength, grew into a measured tread, steadily advanced. A twig snapped, a bough broke, firm steps sounded on the path. The doctor, he'd heard, was on his way!

Relief surging through her, she stood flourishing an arm.

'Over here!' she cried. 'Rosita—she's had a bad fall. Dr Sepulveda, thank heaven . . .'

Mid-sentence, she broke off, stared. Instead of a short dapper figure, she saw a tall rangy one; instead of meeting Lazaro Sepulveda's owl-like gaze, she looked up into Blair Lachlan's amber eyes.

'You! Where did you come from?' she gulped out, amazed.

He jutted his chin. 'A fine reward, for all my hill climbing!' In long strides he reached the injured girl and dropped to his knees.

'How come?' he snapped out.

'I don't know,' Tessa quavered. 'She was in her chair when I left her to gather pinon, looking perfectly safe. When I got back . . .' Staccato, she reported how she'd found her friend.

The doctor ran expert fingers over head, limbs, trunk.

'Beyond that nasty cut, with which you've dealt competently, I find no signs of further injury,' he said. 'But we'll need to check her over, thoroughly. That stone by her head—the one with blood on—that accounts for the wound; I guess she's slightly concussed. We'll get her to the clinic, in the bus; provided she lies flat, there'll be no need for an ambulance. Her chair, where is it? Get it over, pronto!'

'Leave me to do the heaving,' he commanded, when Tessa had done his bidding. As if she were a baby, he lifted the injured girl and tenderly lowered her into her chair. His gentleness touched Tessa, his strength impressed.

'You hold her head, while I do the pushing,' he directed. Carefully, cautiously, he eased the invalid carriage down towards the highway. 'You believe she actually did walk, got that distance on her own two feet?'

'How else?' Tessa struggled to maintain her clasp. 'There's no other explanation. A sudden impulse, it must've been. It's beyond belief, but you saw, as I did . . .'

'H'mmm. A funny thing happened, on the way to picking pinon,' Blair Lachlan mused. 'A girl who couldn't lift a foot, when she started out, managed to get up and walk!'

Tessa threw him a searching glance. 'And someone who wasn't even with the party, at the beginning, suddenly materialised!'

Keeping his gaze on his passenger, the doctor twitched his red lips.

'That can be explained!' he drawled. 'I came out to replace Sep. Earlier today, one of his long-term patients suffered a severe coronary, and the relatives wanted her regular medic in attendance. I drove my car here, lent it to him to get back, stayed on to look after this little crowd; no way would Sep have countenanced them being left without a doctor.'

He grinned. 'Though with you along, I suppose we

needn't have worried—we could have relied on you, to offer your tender care.'

Uncertain whether he was being serious, or sardonic, Tessa decided to give him the benefit of the doubt. Rosita, she must keep Rosita's head steady. Now that she had her in safe keeping, she could relax a little, rejoice. Rosita had walked, that was what mattered.

They occupied one of the long side seats in the coach, with Rosita lying between them, her head cradled on Tessa's lap, her feet against Blair's slim hips. Like a hawk, the doctor watched his patient, kept a rug in place over her.

His back to them, Tony sat on a crosswise bench. Very soon, his head began to droop, then to nod. The doctor jerked a thumb in his direction.

'What beats me is why young Picasso there didn't accompany you up that mountain, give you a hand with the pushing,' he growled. 'Getting Rosita as high as you did must have been quite a struggle.'

Tessa gave a lift of her shoulders. 'Don't worry, Tony did his fair share, earlier on. He worked hard unloading and waited on everybody. When I set off with Ros he was busy drawing, making sketches to give these folk as presents; I didn't care to disturb him.'

A snore vibrated the air. Tony's dark head bobbed down, then jerked up.

'Poor guy!' The drawled comment held sarcasm. 'All that hard work, he's fair worn out!'

Tessa gritted her teeth. 'That's unjust, unkind!' she snapped. 'Leave him alone! A good rest, that's all he needs.'

The amber eyes met hers, the heavy lids lifted.

'That, I do endorse, with all my heart. A long one, I'd recommend!'

CHAPTER NINE

'PINON PICKING OUTING—DISABLED GIRL CRACKS HEAD!
BRITISH NURSE AIDS RESCUE!'

The headline leapt out at Tessa when she opened the newspaper, next morning.

'Now, how did they get hold of that?' she demanded of Ramon, who just entered the dining room.

Reading the item, he frowned. 'Oh, there's always some stringer on hand, anxious to earn the odd dollar. Someone on the outing, the driver, an attendant at the clinic—it could be one of those.'

He smiled. 'Not to worry—all's well that ends well. The latest report on Ros is most reassuring. A day or two's rest in a darkened room, and she'll be okay, Sep says. About the walking, he's completely mystified. Says to maintain a discreet watch, see if she makes another attempt. She's to be allowed home in an hour, and says she'd like to see you.'

Tessa's first thoughts on waking had been for her friend. The previous evening, Rosita had been admitted to the LS immediately on their return, and detained overnight for examination and assessment.

She arrived at Conchita's apartment to find her taking in a cellophaned bouquet from a delivery man.

'For Miss Ruiz,' he was saying. 'No, Ma'am, the sender didn't give a name, only that message, "Wishing you a speedy recovery".'

'How very odd!' Appreciatively, Conchita sniffed the flowers. 'Who could have sent these? Someone on the outing? The church group, maybe? How very kind. Tessa, you take them into Rosita—she's lying on her bed. I hope you can see in there—Laz said she's slightly concussed and we should draw the shades for a while,

151

and for her not to watch TV. Otherwise, she's going on fine—Laz sutured that cut on her head. Thank you, Tessa dear, for all you did, for looking after my one ewe lamb. Such a ghastly shock I got last evening when Blair Lachlan called me. A mercy it was, that things weren't worse. I can't understand what could have happened.'

Rosita blinked up at the bouquet, when Tessa took it in.

'That's for me? You're sure?' she queried. 'The florist hasn't made a mistake, taken "Mrs" to be "Miss"? They're not meant for mama?'

She gave a puzzled frown. 'I don't know a soul who'd send me flowers. And yellow roses—how strange! They're my favourites. Time was . . . Could you find a vase, put it here by my bed?'

She touched her temples. 'My poor head, how it aches! There's a little man in there, I think, laying about him with a big hammer. No, I don't remember what happened up on that hill—all I have is a hazy recollection of trying to stand. That incredible light, it seemed to draw me up, make me feel I could float . . . After that, my mind's a blank; the next thing I knew was a clinic room, a clinic bed. Sep let me look in on Mari on my way out, by the way, to show her I was still in one piece.'

Looking up at the flowers, she furrowed her brow, then winced.

'Who could possibly have sent me roses?'

'That man who sat next to you at the barbecue?' Tessa suggested. 'The car crash victim?'

Rosita sucked in her breath. 'Oh, I do hope not—he was a perfect pill! Actually, it was because of him that I asked you to push me on up—he didn't take his gaze off me, for a moment.'

She sighed. 'It's no use my trying to think, not about anything; Sep advised that I shouldn't. I'm going to shut my eyes, and rest.'

Tiptoeing out, Tessa felt more than a little bewildered.

Obviously, Rosita had managed to take a few steps,

but would she try ever again? Had her confidence been destroyed by the fall, the hard blow on the head? And if she tried and failed, what then? The attempt she had made, did it confirm that she'd been ambulatory all the time, secretly? Stranger things were known. And the renewed desire to walk, what had triggered it? The exciting change of scene, the thrill of being out in the world, or that weird and wonderful light?

To all this speculation there was added an additional riddle. Who was sending Rosita flowers? Not just the one bouquet arrived, but a fresh bunch every day, all that week. Always, they were perfect yellow roses, always they were sent anonymously. Seeking to ascertain the donor's identity, Conchita checked with the florist, but to no avail. The order had been placed by a messenger and paid for by cash in advance, she learned.

The yellow rose mystery, as she came to call it, greatly intrigued the recipient, helped spur on her recovery, brought a sparkle to her eyes. Eagerly Rosita listened every morning for the ring of the doorbell, delightedly exclaimed over each new sheaf. How much longer would the presents continue? To whom was she indebted for them?

'My money's on the guy on the outing,' Tessa confided to her sister. 'There's no doubt he was smitten. Ros is very pretty, so it's not surprising. The pair have similar problems, and maybe something might come of this. Mari, you're not listening. Is anything wrong?'

On her arrival to visit she'd noticed that Marigold looked morose. Thinking to cheer her, she'd related the story of the roses. Still, her sister retained a glum expression.

'You're not feeling too well?' Tessa went to her side.

Marigold sniffed. 'No, and who would be, after hearing the terrible rumour that's buzzing round the clinic, about you and Rae? Put yourself in my place—how would you like to have to lie here, unable to help yourself, and be told by a third party what's going on?'

Tessa took a step back. 'Whatever are you talking

about? What do you mean?'

Eyes blazing, Marigold jerked herself from her pillows. 'I mean you making up to him, and he making up to you; the two of you, carrying on! And not just at home in the apartment, but openly, in public!'

Jaw dropping, Tessa put a hand on her head. 'We've only been out the once—to dinner, at "La Sevilla". Why, yes, I do remember that we fooled about a little, but that was all! Mari, you surely don't believe . . . ?' Aghast, she stared.

Her sister's lips began to twitch, her eyes to twinkle, and she burst into hearty laughter.

'Don't look so upset—I was only teasing!' she gasped out. 'You don't have to have the "fall-aparts"; it was only a leg-pull. I'd trust Rae with you, any old time.'

Tessa heaved a sigh of relief. 'Thank you, thank you very much! But what the hell . . . ? This malicious gossip, where did it start?'

'My question exactly, when "Fish" passed it on; she wanted to alert me. One guess from whence it came?'

Tessa's mind switched back to the restaurant. 'Debra Petersen? She was there with Blair, that evening. But that's ages ago—why this, now?'

'You can't guess? You don't think it possible that a certain someone might have praised your presence of mind last Sunday, your efficiency in coping with Rosita? It could be that a particular lady wasn't too pleased.'

Frowning, Tessa shook her head. 'No-one could be that small-minded, surely? Why, it's pitiable. If it's true . . .'

'If it's true, you'd better be very careful how you tread in future,' Marigold said.

The advice left Tessa wondering. The secretary's jealousy, was it a good omen, or a bad?

Tony, also, showed little interest in the great rose mystery.

'Some nutter's responsible, I guess, someone who read of her accident in the papers,' he suggested. Since the day of the picnic he'd been moody. Having time on her hands during her portrait sitting, Tessa gently prodded to find out the cause.

'There's nothing wrong with me!' he snorted. 'It's you—you're changing! Sunday, what did you do when we got back to Santa Fé? Went rushing straight into the LS with Rosita! Me, you didn't spare a word, not a single backward glance! And all the return journey you stayed with Doc Lachlan. How about the concert we'd planned to attend, that evening?'

'Oh, I forgot all about it! I'm very sorry.' Tessa turned penitent eyes upon him. 'We hadn't booked . . . did it matter? I got caught up at the clinic . . .'

'Keep still, can't you?' he snapped. 'How do you think I can do you justice, painting a moving target?'

From then on, Tessa sat rock still. Something was weighing on Tony's mind, she decided, apart from her forgetfulness. Was Rae increasing the pressure?

Confirmation soon came. The session over, he threw down brush and palette, ran paint-stained fingers through his dark mane.

'Jeepers, but I'd give years of my life to do my own thing!' he exclaimed. 'The moment I attempt to paint what I want, the way I want, up goes the bar! I must produce what'll sell, what the public'll buy, I'm reminded. I hate to be beholden to Rae, as I am. Up to my eyeballs in debt to him, I've no alternative but to do as he wishes. This way, I'll never get places.'

'Oh, but you will—you are doing so,' Tessa hastened to reassure. 'I've every faith in you, and so has Ramon. He's only doing what he thinks best, and he knows the market.'

Throwing up her arms she hugged him hard, gently soothing him. Undoubtedly she'd been most remiss, letting him slip from her mind in the aftermath of the picnic. Remembering the great kindness he'd shown, his thoughtful consideration for everyone on the outing, the assistance he'd rendered, she felt ashamed. Her suggestion, it had been, that he should be one of the company, and she'd neglected to thank him. He couldn't be blamed for feeling hurt. Somehow, she must make recompense, put new heart into him.

Rosita was one person who didn't need cheering. The roses kept coming, and her spirits stayed high. Speculation regarding the sender continued to dominate her thoughts. Several were the sources suggested, the trails followed, without a single clue being unearthed.

Revelation came one full week later, and Tessa was third in line to learn. Calling that fateful Monday to see her friend she found she'd been forestalled. A gentleman was with the mistress and Miss Rosita in the drawing-room, the servant informed her, when she opened the apartment door.

At her entrance a man rose from a chair set close to Rosita, and Tessa found herself staring at a tall thin figure, a head fringed with auburn hair. Gazing up into kind grey eyes, she let out a gasp.

'It's never—I d-don't b-believe it!' Astonishment made her stutter. Before her stood 'Red', the man she'd met at Albuquerque, the man she'd desperately been seeking.

He grinned down. 'Neither did I, when first I realised that the nurse mentioned in that news report was none other than my plane companion! Pleased to renew my acquaintance, Miss Maitland—I'm Earl, Earl Windquist. Beats me how we didn't get round to exchanging names on that flight we shared.'

Me, too, she thought, as he shook her hand vigorously. A great deal of trouble that would've saved. But he looked as nice as she'd remembered, more distinguished even, in his suit of silver grey. Glancing from him to a smiling Rosita, she felt her pulse quicken. Was her dream coming true?

He followed her gaze. 'This lovely lady, such a time I've had tracing her; you'd never believe the half of it!'

Oh, yes, I would, Tessa thought. Knees trembling,

she sank into a chair. You don't know the dance you've been leading me!

'Do tell me . . .' she managed to murmur. At once, simultaneously, they all began to do so, Earl, Rosita, Conchita. The day after he arrived back in New Mexico, the erstwhile suitor had started to seek news of the Ruiz. Though firmly convinced that Rosita had long since married the boy next door, he wanted assurance that things had worked out, that she was happy.

'I'd never been certain, you see, about the sudden change of attitude. But first, there was my new appointment to settle into, and that took a while, and I had to get myself a new car. The previous one I'd traded in, up north. Then . . .'

'Then Earl drove out to our old home,' Rosita broke in. 'Didn't you, darling? What do you think the hacienda is now? A . . .'

'A motel!' Beaming broadly, Conchita couldn't wait to make her contribution. 'A recent conversion, and no-one there knew a thing about us.'

Patiently, Earl Windquist had been waiting to resume his tale. 'Ah, but I eventually found someone who did— an elderly gardener, who'd been kept on by the new owners. It took three visits . . .'

'Juan knew us well, was one of our old "faithfuls",' Conchita interjected. 'He it was who brought Mr Windquist—I mean Earl—up to date, as far as he was able. He informed him of my husband's death, of Rosita's illness . . .'

Pausing, she produced a lace-edged handkerchief. 'That far, the dear old man was right, in what he said. Unfortunately, he went on to report that we'd moved away to the big city; any town's a big city to a peasant, of course.'

'And so Earl was led on a false trail all the way to Albuquerque,' Rosita hastened to explain. 'All the Ruiz listed in the phone book, he called up.'

Earl scratched his domed head. 'And you'll never credit how many scores of them there are! Not until . . .'

'Not until he happened upon the account of the pinon picnic in the paper, spotted it by chance, did he find out we were all here, in Santa Fé!' Conchita put in, dabbing at her eyes.

Like a dedicated spectator at an international tennis finals, Tessa swivelled her head from left to right, from one speaker to the other. Taking in each joyful face, she tingled with happiness. It was too good to be true. Any minute, would she awake from a dream . . . ?

'The roses, they were from you?' she asked, awed.

'Correct!' The red head jerked up and down. 'An idea I hit upon, a warning shot over the bows . . . You see, I'd no wish to come bursting in, after the long separation, give Rosita another shock. Reading of the accident, I at once wanted to send flowers. From that, the notion grew. Way back, I'd always given Ros yellow roses, so I hoped that the bouquets would give the idea I was around once more, ready and waiting. Mid-week, I called Mrs Ruiz, put her in the picture, sought her co-operation.'

'Conchita, please call me Conchita.' Coyly, the request was made.

Tessa shook her head in wonder. A turn-up for the books, that's what Mari's going to call this! This was talking! This was the real way to woo!

'And Earl's not in the least discouraged by this . . .' Rosita gestured downwards, pointed to her legs.

'Why should I be? I'm a "hop-along", aren't I?' He held out his arms. 'These are strong, my shoulders also. Where a car or a wheelchair can't carry you, I will!'

Conchita replaced her handkerchief. 'A short engagement, to make sure about your feelings, that I must insist on. Oh, it's so miraculous—who could've thought this would happen?'

Tessa didn't care to suggest. A lump in her throat, she sat smugly back and rejoiced in the rapture. This was a great day. Her surmise had been proved accurate; 'Red' and Rosita's long lost admirer were one and the same. But Tony had been right too; there'd been no necessity for her to go ferreting about, go to such lengths to sort things out. This blissful pair had not required assistance from her, or from anybody. Determined, devoted, intelligent, Earl Windquist had made it on his own. The wonder was that the couple still held the same affection for each other, and were taking up where they'd left off, three years and more ago. Now, Rosita had every encouragement to make a full recovery, to live life to the full.

Bubbling with excitement, she chose to make an early departure and explained that she must go at once to Marigold to acquaint her with the news.

The time could not have been more opportune, for she found her sister in a state of depression. Her progress had come to a halt; her condition, if anything, had regressed. But she brightened immediately on hearing what Tessa had to tell.

'It's fantastic! I'm thrilled for them both,' she exclaimed. 'Think of it—if all goes well, we could have a family wedding and a christening within the year, and Tess, you'll be in on both.'

Becoming animated, she began to plan. 'We have to think about what to wear for junior's baptism, who's to be invited. When my head stops aching, I'll draw up a list. This incredible news has made me grasshopper minded. Darling Ros, I pray everything goes on coming up roses! If she does marry her Earl, there'll be bonuses—the way'll be clear for Sep and Con. Rae's financial load'll be lightened, and junior'll have an uncle!

'Talking of the infant, could you get on with ordering the nursery equipment? And I'd like the spare room walls freshly colour-washed a peach shade. The room faces north, and that'll lend warmth. For the furnishings, I want duck-egg blue. We'd better get hold of someone who can put the work in hand very soon—I've a strong feeling that young Ruiz isn't going to hang about much longer, waiting to come into this old world.'

Wanting to find someone reliable, Tessa consulted

Tony and he took her, one evening, to call on an interior decorator acquaintance. Shade books examined, an estimate obtained, Tony suggested to Tessa that they should have a quiet dinner.

To her surprise, he led her to the impressive La Fonda, on the Plaza, an historic inn that marked the end of the old Santa Fé trail. After admiring the fascinating blend of Spanish and Indian architecture, Tessa cast Tony an apprehensive glance.

'This place, it looks a mite expensive,' she whispered. 'How about our just taking a drink here, then moving on to eat somewhere more modest?' Somehow, it didn't seem their scene.

He demurred. 'Not tonight,' he said, 'Tonight, we're doing things in style. A cocktail, how about a cocktail? Your choice, what is it?'

They drank Margueritas laced with fresh lime and watched Santa Fé society come and go. A popular meeting place, the hotel was a hive of activity. Did she look sufficiently smart in her sky-blue trouser suit? she wondered. One swift glance around, and she was reassured. Tony confirmed that she'd no cause for concern.

'You look great,' he said, and the gipsy eyes held a long look of yearning; his gaze lingered.

'You look pretty good yourself,' she said with a smile. He had, she observed, dressed with special care. Unusually, his denim suit had been well pressed, and his straight dark hair shone with brushing. As if meeting him for the very first time, she admired the fine olive skin, the coal-black eyes with their dark fringe of lashes, the flattish nose, the chiselled lips, and felt very proud.

When it came to selecting what they'd eat, Tony accepted advice from the waiter and consulted Tessa. Everything was excellent, from the crab cocktail through to fillet mignon with green salad and real strawberry ice-cream.

'Super!' Tessa proclaimed, sipping Grand Marnier with her café au lait. 'Mind you, you shouldn't be spending all this money. But just for a one-off, it's lovely. This kind of thing—it must be kept for special occasions.'

'This is one.' He spoke with deliberation.

'It is? You mean we're here to celebrate for Rosita, mark the return of her Earl?' She giggled. 'Countess, that's what I'm calling her, from now on! Every evening this week, he's taken her for a drive—scooped her up in his arms, plonked her in his car.'

Her eyes gleamed. 'How's that for romance? It's a dream, a dream made real.'

'Uh-huh. And it's seldom that they do.' Wistfully, he regarded her. 'I've never met anyone like you. Your friend's happiness is as near your heart as your own. You're a great girl, Tess; never forget that.'

To reach the cab rank they strolled across the plaza. A cool wind riffled the Chinese elms, and Tony looked up.

'Seems like the wind's shifted north,' he remarked. 'Winter could be coming in. This Indian summer can't last much longer. The colder weather'll limit our getting together.'

'Oh, no, it won't!' Tessa chuckled. 'I've thought about that. Mari's baby'll soon be here, and she'll be wanting to get out and about with Rae once again. Wilma's already made it clear that she's not taking on regular sitting-in, so I'll be offering our services. A comfortable apartment for our meetings, all mod. cons., what could be better?'

He patted her hand. 'You think of everything, my sweet, but I'm not that certain Rae'll welcome the idea.'

All the way back in the cab he sat with his arm about her, her head cradled on his shoulder. Thoughtful, silent, he seemed to savour every second, every minute. And when they parted his kiss was tender, long.

'Remember that I'll always love you,' he said.

Suddenly, it was all happening. For more than two months Tessa had been on tenterhooks, had wondered how it would be when the baby started to come, what time of day the birth would begin.

She caught the distant burr of the telephone bell as she

was dressing next morning, then heard the urgent pad of feet along the corridor. A quick rap came on her door.

'Tessa, it's Mari!' Ramon came bursting in. 'Blair's decided to induce—what a relief! Yesterday, she looked real sick; all the time I was visiting, the staff were in and out maintaining watch. Blair assures me induction's perfectly safe; Mari's condition makes him unwilling to let her go to full-term. The baby should be okay, he says, now that it's up to the thirty-second week.'

Distractedly, he tugged at his collar. 'This damn thing, it's not sitting right.'

Tessa inspected it. 'It'd help if you fastened the buttons through the facing holes—at the moment, they're all askew! Come here—let me do it! Now, do try to stay calm. Babies, remember, get born all the time.'

'Not to Mari, they don't!' Agitatedly, he palmed back his hair. 'I'm going over to her right now. Can you spell me at the clinic, do you think? I'll need to make frequent dashes over to the gallery to keep an eye on the business, and Mari wants one of us with her throughout.'

Tessa started to sweep things into her bag. 'Of course! I'll follow you over as soon as I've seen Wilma and grabbed a cup of coffee.'

She found her sister established in a spotless Labour Ward. A drip had been set in place over the high bed, and Marigold lay watching liquid trickling along the tube taped to her arm.

She nodded up at the bottle. 'The drug in there is to help speed up labour,' she said. 'Thank heaven I'm being started—this can't be over too soon. Blair's promised he won't let it hurt too much, and I'm all set to do lots of deep breathing as soon as contractions begin.'

All day Tessa stayed on hand, helping in whatever way she was able. Tenderly, she sponged her sister's face, gave her cool drinks, provided reassurance.

'To think our poor mother went all through this!' Marigold groaned, after a spasm of pain. 'I never realised . . .'

The nurse in attendance smiled. 'No woman does, not

until they've experienced parturition. The strange thing is that once over, the pain's entirely forgotten: only the pleasure gets remembered, the pleasure of seeing and handling a newborn child. Why, we have one patient who regularly declares "Never again!" while in labour, and yet within the year she's back here to produce another small son or daughter!'

'She's welcome!' Marigold gritted her teeth. 'You can count me out!'

The hours dragged by. Masked and gowned figures came and went. Though all of them were calm, all very competent, Tessa felt her confidence soar whenever Blair Lachlan looked in. He had about him an aura, the aura she'd observed about all first-class medical men; his presence ensured that a patient was left in no doubt, was given faith in a satisfactory outcome. The dogmatism that made him appear dictatorial as a man gave him authority as a doctor. Without raising his voice one iota, without making the slightest fuss, he commanded immediate respect.

Marigold grew wan as the day wore on, looked all eyes, became impatient. The standard comment continually bestowed upon her started to irritate.

'"You're doing nicely!" That's all anyone can say!' she complained. 'If this is nicely, then I'd hate to be doing poorly!'

After he'd closed the gallery Ramon came hurrying in, offering to take over from Tessa until morning. She agreed to go for a meal, but found she couldn't face the food when it was served, anxiety depriving her of appetite. Returning to the LS, she persuaded Ramon to get himself a supper. He came back red-cheeked and blowing on his hands.

'The temperature's falling fast, and the sky's like lead,' he reported. 'Tessa, I insist you get on home—find a cab while there's one on the street; the weather looks like cutting up rough, and if it does, taxis'll be difficult to come by.'

He sighed, and taking her by the arm, he led her into

the corridor. 'There's no knowing how long this is going on,' he confided. 'It could be a while yet, I gather. As soon as there's news, I'll call you. Meantime, one of us should get some shut-eye.'

Though she didn't admit it to Ramon, Tessa had been growing concerned about her sister; she sensed a disappointment among the staff at the protraction of the birth. Still, it was a first baby . . . It was with a heavy heart that she returned to the apartment. Would Mari be all right? Would the baby be fit and healthy? Her body got into bed, but her mind stayed back at the clinic.

Unable to get to sleep, she picked up an Agatha Christie whodunnit and gazed at the unread words until they blurred. Vaguely, she was conscious of the novel sliding to the floor with a thump . . .

The thump repeated, grew loud, persistent. Blinking, she sat up, saw her bedside light still on, that it was four-thirty. The thump came again, at her door.

'Miss Tessa! Wake up, please! The master, he's on the phone!' Wilma was shouting. 'The baby—I think it's been born.'

At first, the receiver slipped from her fingers and had to be retrieved. Picking it up, she caught the sound of heavy breathing.

'Ramon?' she asked, urgently.

High-pitched, her brother-in-law's voice trembled the line.

'It—it's a b-baby—a b-boy,' he stuttered. 'Five pounds over!' Tessa's throat tightened; tears welled into her eyes.

'Mari?' she whispered. 'She's okay?'

'Fine, just fine—and the boy. Our son, I saw h-him come into the world! Such an experience—I c-can't tell you . . . Now, I'm starting for home—be with you soon.'

Giving a great gasp of relief, Tessa put down the phone. It was over, and all was well! Filled with happiness, she felt tears well into her eyes. Mari and Rae had a son, she had a nephew, her parents a grandchild! Life went on . . . life was wonderful!

Turning, she bumped straight into Wilma. Sleeping cap awry, nightdress tightly clutched, the housekeeper made the sign of the cross against her breast.

'I heard! A new little Ruiz, a son and heir! Thanks be to God, for a safe delivery! I'm that happy, I could cry!'

Straight away she burst into tears and threw her arms about Tessa. Hugging one another, they did a little dance of joy and wept together.

'I'll not get to sleep again,' Wilma said, when she'd dried her eyes. 'I'll go and fix us some tea.'

Barely had Tessa regained her room than the phone started to buzz a second time. She raced to answer it.

'Sorry, Tess, to bother you,' Ramon said, his voice now calm. 'But I'm in a spot. My car won't start. You mayn't know it, but it's snowing like crazy—lying a foot deep, out on the forecourt. With all the recent hassle, I didn't give a thought to anti-freeze. Seems I'm not the only one caught out—there's not a cab to be had.'

She heard him clear his throat. 'Could you drive down and pick me up, do you think? Get the night porter to dig out Mari's Mercedes? Housed in a heated garage, that should start first go. I'm dead on my feet, or I'd walk. I'll be waiting in the vestibule.'

He rung off before she could speak, find words. Open-mouthed, she stared down at the dial. How to call him back, explain she was terrified? That she'd found the big car baffling to handle in good weather, in daylight, so how would she get on in heavy snow, by night? But even as a nervous shiver ran through her at the very thought of trying, a picture flashed into her mind, a picture of Ramon waiting patiently at the clinic, weary, drooping, and she knew she hadn't the heart to refuse, not after his long worrying vigil. In a few hours he had to open the gallery, be on parade for his clients, look dapper, alert. He needed sleep, and she must go to his rescue.

At once, she rang Reception, asked for the car to be brought round. Dressing in a jump-suit, she pulled on an anorak.

'Miss Tessa, you're never going out at this time of the

morning?' Appearing with a laden tray, Wilma turned wide eyes upon her. 'It's snowing, did you know?'

Tessa shrugged. 'Someone's got to chauffeur the proud father—his car's given up! That tea'll have to wait, I fear.'

Making for the door, she tossed a parting remark over her shoulder. 'And by the time we get back, it's brandy we'll need, I'm thinking!'

The night security man carefully guided the car beneath the portico, brought it to the door, left the engine running.

'Lovely picture, the snow makes,' he remarked, as he climbed out.

'One I prefer to see on Christmas cards,' Tessa commented, sliding behind the wheel. 'On a night like this, I'd prefer to stay in bed. But there, this is a small price to pay, I suppose, for acquiring a nephew. The controls, how do they go?—can you remind me?'

The security man flicked her a security man glance.

'You have a nephew? Now, ain't that dandy! I'll take you from left to right, along the dash-board.' He spoke quickly, seeming anxious to get away.

Thick and fast, the snow came slanting at the car, dotted the windscreen with dollar-size flakes until Tessa could scarcely see out; the clean curves swept by the strong wipers were instantly re-layered. Everywhere, everything, glistened white; roads, sidewalks, roofs; every tree had turned a Christmas symbol overnight.

Beneath the soft blanket the town lay slumbering, and Tessa was truly thankful. At least, there were no other motorists about to hinder or to scare. Until she encountered a gritting lorry near the town centre she didn't set eyes on another vehicle.

Body tense, eyes burning, she drove up to the LS entrance, brought the Mercedes to a kangaroo halt, hurried into the vestibule.

Huddled into a big armchair, Ramon sat blissfully snoring. Tessa had to shake him, to wake him up.

'Who—what—where am I?' he waffled, squinting one

eye. 'Oh, Tess, it's you—hello, there. A fine bouncing boy . . . Alvaro Peter, he's being called . . . the two grandfathers . . .' Slurred, his words were puffed out, and he seemed about to collapse back into sleep.

Steps sounded on the tiles; a tired drawl came from behind.

'Come along, my friend, let me help you up. It's high time we both took a rest.'

Still white-gowned, Blair Lachlan stepped forward, assisted Ramon to his feet, then to the door. Outside, his gaze went from the car to Tessa.

'You drove here in the Mercedes? Through this snow?' he asked, in astonishment. The amber eyes flicked approval. 'That's my girl!'

Despite the crisp cold, she felt a warm glow. Again, he'd given praise, used those heart-stopping words; like an accolade, they came.

'I've still to get back,' she pointed out, as she settled behind the wheel.

'You'll manage!' The wide lips slanted in a smile. 'But don't forget to drive on the right! Over here, remember, we drive on the civilised side!'

There never was such a baby, if his parents were to be believed. Though to his aunt Alvaro Peter appeared just another scarlet-faced, kitten-eyed newborn, to his doting mother and father he was without peer. Marigold maintained that he was the image of his handsome father, Ramon that it was his lovely mother he favoured.

The pair were somewhat overloud in their praises, Tessa decided. All the same, the tiny bundle brought out in her a deep protective instinct, and she longed to hold him, to show him off to Tony. He liked children, and she was positive he'd like Alvaro Peter. Would her babies have crumpled rose faces?

For Tessa, the first morning was packed with action and excitement. There was a joyous visit to the clinic, a phone-call to her parents in England that left her choked with emotion, friends of the Ruiz to be contacted and informed, a birth announcement to be conveyed to the local newspaper, flowers to be ordered. Ramon himself carried the good news to his mother and Rosita.

Pleasantly exhausted, Tessa returned to the apartment soon after midday and made herself comfortable on the settee in the lounge. Kicking off her shoes, she closed her eyes. Forty winks, and she'd feel fine. The pressure was off; no-one immediately needed her.

A light touch roused her from her doze. Blinking up, she saw Ramon staring down, and shook herself into consciousness.

'You've come back for a bite of lunch?' she asked, in surprise. 'Shall I go and let Wilma know?'

Slowly, he shook his head. 'No need—I've seen her; she's fixing some sandwiches. Actually, it's you I came to see . . .'

He cleared his throat. 'I'm afraid I have bad news . . .'

Instantly, she was all attention; the strained expression, the taut stance, impinged. She jerked up.

'Mari—not Mari? The baby . . . Something's gone wrong?'

For a split second, the corners of his mouth lifted. 'No—they're in good shape—it's not them.' He tugged at his beard. 'I'm sorry, I should've made that plain straight away—I'm not doing this too well.'

The faint smile had flickered out. 'It's Tony . . .'

Her heart stood still. 'An accident . . .? He's ill . . .?' Her worst fear, she couldn't bring herself to utter. Clenching her fists, she felt her nails scrape her skin. 'He's not . . .' A gulp took away her voice.

'No, no! It's quite different . . . Nothing physically disastrous . . .' He rubbed his brow. 'I don't know how to tell you. Maybe a drink would help us both—yes, I'll pour two brandies.' Turning, he moved towards the cocktail cabinet.

She swung her legs to the floor, floundered after him.

'Oh, no—tell me first, please. I want to know, I must know, now! What's happened to Tony?'

He threw out his arms. 'He's gone, cleared out, vamoosed!'

She swayed back. 'He couldn't have—he'd have said . . .' Desperately, she sought a reason. 'A day or two off, to paint a landscape, that's what he's taking . . .'

Wearily, Ramon sighed. ''Fraid not—His possessions have been removed, and he left me a note—it says he's not coming back! An hour ago I found it, when I called over to the studio, to tell him about our baby. His message asked that I should look after you and expresses regret for letting me down. There was a letter for you, too, I have it here. Let me get you a chair, pour you a drink, then you shall have it.'

Her fingers trembled as she took the square of folded sketch paper and opened it. Written in crayon, the words sloped unevenly, the letters were ill-formed.

Her blood running cold, she read the smudged scrawl.

'Tess, my sweet,' the message ran. 'By the time you receive this, I'll be gone from Santa Fé, gone from your life for ever. You're far too good for me, always were. I think I realised that, right from our first evening to-gether, but it was love at first sight. I love you still, and that's why I'm leaving; it's for your sake. To go on like we are would mean hurting you more, in the long run. I've been reaching for the moon, fooling myself that I could lift myself to your level. It's not fair to keep you from others, the way I've been doing, to keep you from better men. Try to remember me kindly; I shall never forget you. Believe me, this is all for the best; don't try to find me. With all my heart, I wish you happiness.' In capitals, he'd drawn his signature, 'TONY'.

A lump blocked her throat. She swallowed, gulped, watched a tear splash down on to the stiff paper. Clearly, she could see Tony crouched over a littered table, labori-ously writing, could picture his swarthy face twisting in distress, the gipsy eyes narrowing with pain.

Poor dear gentle Tony; he had tried, how he had tried! A simple soul from a simple background, he'd found the sophisticated world too much for him, too strange. That dinner at La Fonda, it'd been his gesture of farewell. If only she'd realised, helped him more . . .

Tear followed tear, made little runnels on the letter that shook in her hand; she gave a gasping sob.

An arm went round her shoulders, briefly held her.

'I'll be in my study,' she heard Ramon say huskily. 'I guess you'd prefer to be on your own, for a while.'

'Maybe I did push him a little too hard,' he said, some time later, over the snack lunch Wilma had prepared. 'But it was with the best of intentions, for his own good; I was ambitious on his account. Now, I feel terrible, but one does what seems best . . . Time, you must give yourself, time, Tess, to get over this; people say it's the great healer. It's for you that I'm most concerned.'

He pushed forward the plate of tuna fish sandwiches.

'You won't try these? Not just one? Ah, well . . . I hate to rub it in, but Tony was never that steady . . . It was a big challenge for a pueblo boy, breaking into competitive art. Which is, I imagine, what brought about his big problem.'

His gaze met Tessa's, and she knew that he read the unspoken question.

'The drink—you didn't know? Weren't aware of the vodka jags? Cleverly, he concealed them—I didn't cotton on till recently. And this morning when I took a look round the back of the studio, there was a knee-high mound of empty bottles. His unpredictability, moodiness, short absences, lack of discipline, the liquor could explain all those.'

He stroked his beard. 'Right from the start, I was uneasy about your association, blamed myself for inviting him to your party, but that day when I glanced in on him he was looking more than usually lonely. With you around, he smartened up, made greater effort, and I began to hope he'd make something of himself, use that considerable talent, get ahead. Even so, I didn't care for the way you were getting involved. Mari and I, we did our best to warn, but folk in love don't hear that well.'

Her heart had been sinking, sinking, sinking. With a shaky finger, she circled the edge of her table mat.

'The money he owed you—is it a big loss?' she asked, in a whisper.

He spread his hands. 'A year's subsidising, that's all—nothing to worry about. What is the loss of money, compared to the breaking of a heart?' He lowered his voice. 'Though my hope is, Tess, that you'll find you've suffered only a slight crack, one that'll heal when you get over the shock.'

He tilted his head. 'Anyway, with so much going for me, who am I to complain? I've a fine new son, a beautiful wife who'll now get fit and strong. Ros looks like making out with her man of science, and mama has a starry gaze in her eyes whenever she's with Sep! My financial commitments seem like diminshing for a bit—that is, till Alvaro starts school. No, you're the one who needs a hand right now, but very soon that young man and his mother'll be home, and you'll be fully occupied. Meanwhile, count on me to be around. Care to come with me now, to the gallery? A little too soon? Then expect me back when we close, and we'll visit Mari together, dine out after, if you like.'

He looked back, from the door.

'By the way, the one thing Tony did leave was his portrait of you—he pinned your name to it. I left it on my dresser. Take a look if you wish; if not, it doesn't matter.'

She sat hunched on her chair after he'd gone, feeling too weak to move. The bottom had dropped from her world and she was numb, numb with shock. Her thoughts were on Tony. Where had he gone? What would he do? Had he sought refuge with Inez? With her, he'd be cared for, be loved.

Eventually, she managed to rise, stagger towards her room along the corridor. The door to Marigold's suite stood wide, and through the gap she sighted the square of canvas perched on Rae's dressing-chest. She hesitated, took a few steps, then went back, curiosity conquering.

Cautiously, she approached the picture, met herself face to face, stared at her likeness in paint. The sensation she experienced was uncanny, disturbing. It was her, yet it wasn't. The eyes were the right shade of blue, and the face and mouth were correctly shaped. Her straight hair, that was how it hung; the nose, that had an upward tilt.

So, what was it that was wrong? A close study, and she knew. The portrait was idealised, too good to be true; the face in the picture had a glossy beauty that the original didn't possess, a calendar-cover perfection. And it was as perfect as Tony had seen her, both as a painter and as a man. And she had seen him that very same way.

'Love makes one blind,' hadn't someone said? Slowly, deliberately, she turned the canvas to face the wall. Ramon could keep it, sell it in the gallery, put the money received towards recouping his loss. But her loss, how could she compensate for that?

Tears streaming, she threw herself on her bed and cried out her heart, sobbing away her great sorrow.

CHAPTER TEN

PURPOSEFULLY, Tessa made her way towards the clinic. Ten days, ten long days, had passed since Tony's flight, and gradually she'd come to terms with life. The adjustment had been far from easy; over and over, she'd relived those shared weeks, reviewed the close relationship. In the analysis, incidents had surfaced from her subconscious, revealing indications of stress ignored or overlooked at the time, and these had tormented her.

More alert, more observant, more considerate, could she have helped Tony better? Picked up clues as to his problem, assisted him to solve it? The increased moodiness, the diminished interest in food, the inability to cope with work systematically, the signs and symptoms had all been there, were obvious, with hindsight. The talent had existed, the forethought, the gentleness; there'd been so much that was good in Tony. Was it to be wasted?

The sadness lingered, but resignation had replaced resentment and despair. His farewell note had held a ring of truth. Right from the start there'd been too much against them, too many differences. She'd been warned, but had chosen not to listen. Her fault, as much as Tony's, the final reckoning . . .

'Better to discover now, than later,' Mari had consoled. Strangely, it had been the portrait more than anything, more than anyone, that had brought her to her senses. Very clearly, it had revealed that Tony had been in love with an illusion, not with flesh and blood. And she, hadn't she similarly projected upon him her own ideal of a man, seen him as she wanted to see him, not as he really was? The affection she'd borne him had been supportive, protective, more that of a mother for a child than a woman for a man; without pausing for thought, she'd rushed to his defence when he'd been criticised, taken up the fight on his behalf. That kind of love wouldn't have sufficed, in the long run.

Cut to the quick though she had been, Tessa kept a corner for him, in her heart. There was so much that she owed him. His admiration, his appreciation, had given her self-confidence, better self-knowledge and enabled her to feel she could keep up with Marigold. Still, her thoughts frequently turned to Tony. How was he, and where? The pity of his plight deeply touched her. Could a talent endangered by drink survive? Could he make a fresh start, prosper? With the help of one of his own kind, with the help of Inez, it wasn't impossible.

Since that dreadful day when Ramon had delivered the hateful news, she'd gone all out to occupy her time. Thankfully, there'd been plenty to do—the spare room to convert into a nursery for Alvaro Peter, new curtains to sew, furniture to purchase. Marigold had kept her on the go, had requested that she write the 'Thank you' notes for all the flowers and gifts that had poured into the LS for mother and son. Wilma had sought her assistance with household requirements, having in mind the imminent arrival home of her mistress. By existing from day to day, hour to hour, minute to minute, Tessa had managed to blanket out her misery.

But the desolation did still hit hard at times. Watching Marigold with Ramon, Rosita with Earl, Conchita with Sep, she was aware of a deep inner longing for someone of her own. The shock she'd sustained had led her to a resolution. Next time, it must be a different kind of loving, the love of a grown woman for a grown man, a man who could command her respect.

Carefully, she picked a path through the slush patterning the sidewalk. On the roads and sidewalks the snow had messily melted, but on the roofs of the rose-pink houses it remained smooth and white; it looked like frosting on strawberry cake. A chill wind riffled the few vein-bared leaves, and she turned up the collar of her anorak. Sensibly, she'd donned a red sweater and matching woollen slacks and tucked the trousers into knee-high black boots.

Sighting the LS she knew a mix of emotions, for this was to be her last regular visit to the clinic. Tomorrow, Marigold was due home, with her baby. In one way, she was relieved that this was the final trek; in another, she was sorry. For weeks, the clinic had figured large in her life; it was hard to believe it would do so no longer.

The release from daily visiting she saw as a blessing and as a loss. She would miss the hospital atmosphere for it was one in which she felt truly at home and she liked chatting with the staff. She enjoyed meeting Dr Sep, Nurse Fisher, the nurses, and also Blair Lachlan who was a continual challenge.

The staff gossip, too, was entertaining. Right up to the last, Debra Petersen was providing interest, for tongues had been set wagging by the degree of attention she was paying the new doctor. According to 'Fish', general opinion was that the man was being used as a pawn to capture a knight, the knight being Blair Lachlan, the goal being checkmate at the altar, the object being to spur on the suitor.

Would she, would she not, be successful? Inexplicably, the thought sent a stab of pain across Tessa's temples. Turning in between the high gates, she saw a white wagon, side-signed with a large red cross, lumber out from the forecourt, labour round a corner, slow to a halt by the kerb. Why stop so short a distance from its starting point by the clinic portico, she idly wondered.

A shout assailed her ears. Glancing sideways, she saw a hand flapping through an open window at the front of the cab. The driver must be needing direction. Running along the sidewalk, she peered up.

'Can I be of assistance . . .' she asked, then caught her breath. 'You? What on earth . . .'

Blair Lachlan grinned down. 'No time to explain—I'll do so as we go along. The answer to your question is yes, I have need of one nurse.'

Clicking open the door, he swung it wide.

'Hop in, and make it snappy,' he ordered. 'I've no time to waste!'

Bewildered, Tessa gazed up. 'But Mari—she's expecting me!'

'No, she's not! I saw to that! Told her I'd get on my way to find you, the moment I heard you were heading for the LS. No need to worry about that sister of yours—right now, she has that precious son of hers clamped to a lovely breast, and all day there'll be visitors streaming in and out. You'll not be missed. Jump in, I said!'

She knew a sudden indignation. This ordering about, it was too much!

'Why should I?' she demanded, eyes flashing. 'First, I'd like to be told . . .'

Her words were drowned by the crashing back of the driver's door. In a twinkling the doctor had dropped down on to the pavement. Hands gripping like a vice round her slim waist, he hoisted her high, lowered her on to the long bench seat, and climbed up beside her.

'I'll put you in the picture on the way,' he said, slamming the door. 'From now on, I'll need to shout—this diesel engine makes one hell of a din.'

Rattling, shaking, the wagon curved out into the line of traffic

'Now, I want to know NOW!' Tessa furiously bellowed. 'Where . . . ? Why . . . ? What . . . ?'

'You're going to make yourself useful for a change, that's what!' he yelled back. 'Today, it's my turn for a stint of doctoring up at a pueblo, and my sessional nurse has let me down. Every time one of her kids takes sick this happens, but previously I've had a 'floater' nurse who could help me out. That day we met up at "Los Arboles", I was about to ask if you'd be willing to stand in on an occasion such as this, but that doorman hauled me off. You had no appointments, nothing better to do today, I learned from Marigold, so don't try to tell me you're being inconvenienced. You surely can't object to sparing a little time for some needy Navajo, lending a hand at a mother and baby clinic?'

'So now you ask!' Her voice rose shrill. 'Kidnapping's a serious offence, let me tell you. What if I scream, call over the policemen at the cross-roads? You'll look pretty silly.'

'Scream on!' He was smiling, a lop-sided mischievous grin. 'You're no kid, so come off it! And the cops here are all good friends—I'll insist that you're a stowaway. Sit back, relax, feel flattered that you've been asked along! Remembering how you pride yourself on your profession, I imagined you'd be delighted to have this opportunity! Despite all my warnings, you insisted on employing your skill on that scatterbrained sister of yours—today'll be much more rewarding!'

They'd halted at a traffic signal. An amused expression slanting his red lips, he sat studying her. She remarked the springy tawny curls, the lean sunburnt cheeks, the roguish glint in the amber eyes. He's a devil, this man, she thought.

Large, capable, his hands played pit-a-pat on the rim of the steering wheel; watching the slender fingers she remembered the strength of his touch.

'Having had time to reflect about Marigold's setback, I guess I was over-hasty in blaming you,' he drawled unexpectedly.

The light changed to green, and he let in the clutch.

'This clinic we're staging, it's routine stuff.' He raised his voice above the engine roar. 'You, I take it, can manage to weigh a few babies, enter up records, help mothers disrobe when necessary, hand out infant foods?'

He jerked his head back, indicating the rear of the wagon.

'The necessary equipment's all there, everything required to set up shop. This jalopy's owned by a charity, given out on loan to whichever medic happens to be on voluntary duty. Any questions?'

She was left speechless, unable to think of a thing to

ask. The engine rumble didn't aid concentration.

'Lunch,' she pronounced, after a pause. 'In a pueblo, where do we eat? Should I buy something, before we run out of shops?'

Benevolently, he bowed. 'I don't mind you sharing my dinner pail!'

Indignation subsiding, interest aroused, Tessa leant back on the hard seat. This, of all things! One minute she'd been strolling along, minding her own business; the next, she was being whirled off in a noisy wagon to the hills! What a nerve Blair Lachlan had! But a pueblo visit would be an experience, an uncommon chance. Initially, her reaction had to be to leap out the first time the vehicle was obliged to halt; now, she was pleased that she hadn't done so.

She watched the firm fingers swing the heavy wheel a full circle.

'Learnt to handle one of these in Vietnam,' he flung out, observing her glance. 'One of those extra skills it pays to pick up in such a situation, just in case . . . My best buddy, another medic, and I, we both of us did. Sadly, he didn't live long enough to do much driving. The bomb with his number on deprived me of a good pal, and Debra of a good husband.'

'Debra?' At once, she was all ears. 'She was married to an army man, a Dr Petersen?'

A nod preceded a shake of his head. 'Yes, to the first, No, to the second question. Tex was her first husband, Petersen her second. Him, I didn't know. Sadly, the subsequent marriage didn't work. Deb plunged into a second go too soon after losing Tex, I guess, out of loneliness. Partly, I was to blame, I fear; I was at fault.'

The city was thinning out; houses were being replaced by fields and trees. In the open country the big engine seemed to reverberate even louder. Shaking the cab, the vibrations quivered Tessa's body and enhanced her awareness of the virile figure beside her.

Intrigued by what Blair had revealed, she edged forward.

'Your fault?' she queried.

'Yep! If I'd got there sooner . . . You see, after Tex was hit, he lasted out some hours. With his dying breath he begged me to go and visit his wife when I got back, help her over the worst patch, act as a prop, see that she didn't make any rash decisions.'

He touched his scarred cheek. 'Well, what with collecting this little graze and getting hospitalised, it was some while before I could fulfil the pledge I'd given. Meantime, the Petersen guy had seized his chance and prevailed on Deb to remarry. When the match didn't gel, he lit out. My visit came too late; all it did was to deepen Deb's sense of loss. She badly needed a job and a change, I needed a secretary. That's how she came to move to Santa Fé and join us at the LS. That period in time, we were both of us in a mess; two ways, the plan worked.'

The road rose steep, the engine banged and roared; Blair's drawl was overlaid with deafening noise. She saw the full lips move, but couldn't catch the words. Soon, he gave up the attempt to talk, gave a wry smile, a despairing shrug.

Puzzled, she sat back. Why this sudden burst of confidence? Why bother to make the explanation? The announcement of his own wedding, was that where the chat was leading?

Her heart gave a lurch. Already, he was half-way up the aisle. What a snare sympathy could prove; before you knew where you were, it had you in its toils. That's how it'd been with her and Tony. Debra Petersen wasn't right for Blair. Now that she knew the doctor better, knew his warmth, his sincerity, she was certain that the secretary was too cold, too superficial.

The diesel drummed on and the drone hurt her ears. How much further?

A fork appeared in the road, and Blair Lachlan swung the wagon into the righthand lane; the rough track wound between snow dappled fields. A wintry sun silvered the backdrop of mountains and lit the blue sky;

skeletal, charcoal-black, tall trees stood like cardboard cut-outs. It was a dramatic landscape, bare, stark.

A mile or so on and the winding lane debouched into a broad clearing fringed with small adobe dwellings. A large wooden hut centred the area and its porch carried a signboard: 'SCHOOL'.

'We get loaned a room here,' Blair Lachlan said, driving up to the front steps. 'By the look of that waiting line, we've got ourselves a busy day.'

Burdened with babies and infants, dark-skinned women were squatting in a long row on the roofed verandah. Dressed in plush blouses and velvet skirts in rich fruit shades, their shoulders draped with bright serapes, their raven plaits topped by high crowned sombreros, they looked as colourful as flowers in a summer garden.

At a blast from the wagon, a crowd of sloe-eyed children came padding from a classroom. Shepherded by a vigilant teacher, they helped unload, wheeling in an examination couch, a screen, a trolley carrying scales, files, boxes. Rapidly, the room allocated to the visitors took on a clinical appearance. No sooner had doctor and nurse donned white overalls than they were in business, aided by a teacher turned interpreter.

It didn't take Tessa long to realise why her assistance had been deemed necessary; the case-load was formidable. So much for Blair's 'few babies', she thought, as she counted more than forty.

Of necessity, progress was slow. Time had to be allowed for translation, and for the removal of layers of clothing. Reluctantly, the mothers requiring examination shed as few garments as they could and insisted on retaining their tall hats even when requested to lie flat. With some difficulty, Tessa managed to repress her amusement.

On sight, she fell in love with the babies. Weighing them, marking up their progress charts, she had time to admire their coal-black eyes, rosebud mouths, honey-coloured skin; to her, they looked like oriental dolls.

Blair Lachlan, she observed, also found them enchanting. Proceeding unhurriedly, he paid close attention to each and every one, paused to coax a smile here, tickle a small palm there. But it was his sympathetic treatment of a month-old boy with a hare-lip that moved her almost to tears. The child held high, hard against his broad chest, he bent his head, lightly touched the disfigured mouth with his lips. Infinitely patient, immeasurably kind, he assured the anxious mother that the ugly defect could be, and would be, corrected by surgery.

Near to choking, Tessa had to avert her gaze and quickly draw her cuff across her misted eyes. A great wave of emotion rose within her; at that moment she knew she loved him. That wound that had scarred him and left him over-sensitive, had also made him perceptive to the suffering of others. How was it that she had so misjudged him?

Half-way through the long list they took a break and carried the mugs of hot chocolate that willing hands had brought them out on to the balcony, together with Blair's box of sandwiches. After the stuffiness of the medical room, the fresh air came as a tonic. Tessa took deep breaths.

'Take care,' Blair warned. 'This dry cold can be deceiving—the temperature's lower than you'd think. You need a coat.'

Fetching her anorak, he draped it round her shoulders. The touch of his hands sent a tingle running through her. That Debra Petersen should be so lucky, she thought; what a waste of a good man!

'Our patients don't share our obsession with washing,' he was saying. 'Often, they lack the water. Given a lead, they respond well to training and are highly intelligent. They readily accept immunisation, and there's been a notable drop in preventable diseases.'

He chewed on a sandwich. 'The difficulty comes when these folk try to make the transition from their way to our way of life—the gap's enormous. Some of the brightest, even, don't succeed.'

His gaze met hers. 'An artist I know found the challenge too formidable and was driven to seek solace in the bottle, and then to escape . . .'

Her heart stood still. So he knew, had heard, about Tony . . . Hadn't mentioned him by name, out of consideration.

He cleared his throat. 'On the surface, this man had a lot going for him—looks, talent, charm, but there was an underlying lack of confidence, a feeling of not knowing who he was, of not belonging; hence the drinking.'

The drawl softened. 'I longed to warn you, to urge caution, that first evening, when I saw you dancing, being paid such avid attention. Anyone else possessing the same knowledge could have, but medical etiquette seals a doctor's lips, so far as patients are concerned.'

He gave a wry smile. 'I did all I could, followed the instinct that drove me, did my damndest to cut in—and a lot of good that did! All the effort I made to get better acquainted, to have Anna and Vance invite me along when you were their guest got me nowhere. Single-minded you started, and single-minded you stayed, though your lips gave me hope, festival night. A lot of valuable time's been wasted . . .'

You can say that again! Staring, she almost uttered the challenge; but for his quick movement, she might have done.

Flinging out an arm, he gestured towards the entrance.

'Jeepers, just look at that crowd forming up for attention! It's back to work, or we'll never get through, this side of tomorrow. Quick march, Tessa Maitland!'

Let them wait! she wanted to cry, seeing him stamp off; wait, till you've explained! Was it true, what he'd said? The party invitations, had he purposefully obtained them? If so, why? Out of loyalty to Mari and Rae? For what other reason . . . ?

Heart thumping, mind whirling, she followed in his striding wake, shakily resumed her station at the weighing machine. Only the discipline she'd acquired during her years of training kept her methodically working, undressing babies, balancing them on the scales, scribbling figures.

Her gaze kept flicking to the window. Facing west, it showed the slow descent of the November sun, the crimsoning of sky. The morning had flown, but the afternoon seemed interminable. When would the clinic end?

Across the room the doctor worked calmly on, seemingly unaware of her frequent glances. What went on she wondered, in that handsome high head. What had driven him to act the way he said he had? And why the revelation? Tantalised, confused, she ached to find out.

By the time the last patient plodded away, purple dark was dulling the crimson dusk. Their gear reloaded, they climbed into the wagon, waved their farewells, drove from the pueblo.

Now, Tessa was more than ever aware of the powerful figure seated beside her, of the strong arms that swung the heavy steering, of the sinewy thighs and long muscular legs that stretched to manipulate clutch and brake; every nerve in her seemed to twitch, every inch of flesh to tingle.

And yet, she felt a hollowness, a void. Too late, she had seen, marked, learned. Given her New Mexican time over again, she'd seize with both hands all those missed opportunities. Mari had been right, all along. This was no ogre at her side; this was a giant among men, heart, soul, body.

Yet it was a giant with a fault. Maddeningly, Blair Lachlan started to hum a pop tune as soon as they hit the highway, went on to whistle through his shining white teeth. It came as a relief when he stopped, peering through the windscreen.

'I'm looking out for "The Whispering Waterfall,"' he shouted, above the engine din. 'It's a roadhouse, a pretty good restaurant. We'll eat there. Those sandwiches we shared weren't sufficient to satisfy a fledgling. You've earned your chow, Tessa Maitland.

Ah, here's the neon sign, coming up now.'

She caught his arm. 'But I have to get back—Mari's expecting me . . .'

'Then let her expect on! For once, think of yourself, not your sister!'

'But—but I ought to let her know . . .'

'And so you shall, Tessa Maitland. This, may I remind you, is a fairly advanced country; we have telephones, even in the restaurants! Bell invented it here, remember? So you'll call Marigold, tell her where you are. Same time, I'll call the office, advise Debra to shut up shop—that is, if she still happens to be around. These days, she doesn't hang about, like she used to. That new doc . . . Hold on to your seat, I'm diving off this highway, and the road's kind of bumpy.'

Rattling in to the parking lot, he hauled on the brake and switched off the engine. Striding to the passenger door, he opened it, reached in, picked her up, swung her to the ground. His hands lingered on her waist, sending a shiver of desire rising.

'The phone booths are by the entrance,' he directed, guiding her up a flight of steps. 'See you!'

He stood lounging against a pillar when she folded back the door, arrogantly confident. Outstandingly handsome, he looked captivating, prepossessing. Sincerely, she wished she'd not been so blind for weeks, for months.

'Okay?' he enquired. 'You may stay out late? Me, too. My call didn't take so long—Deb was anxious to be off.'

He took hold of her arm, running his hand slowly down.

'I've ordered champagne, so that we can celebrate.'

She stared up. 'Celebrate? Celebrate what?'

A teasing smile tilted the corners of the sensuous mouth.

'An engagement—one that's about to be announced.'

She felt her blood run cold. How could she pretend? Fake pleasure she couldn't feel?

'But—but shouldn't you be doing that with—with your fiancée?'

He gave an emphatic jerk of his head, tossing forward a tawny curl.

'You're so right! That is exactly my intention!'

Her heartbeats quickened and she felt her face colour.

'I—I don't understand . . . You and Debra, surely . . . That evening at "La Sevilla", didn't you get engaged then? I thought . . .'

He threw back his head, opened his mouth, bellowed a guffaw.

'Then you thought wrong! Tessa Maitland, you shouldn't jump to conclusions! That "Sevilla" dinner was by way of being a signing-off, not a signing on! A civilised "thank-you-and-let's-be-good-friends" occasion! I needed to get the message over loud and clear, to halt the drifting. . . . Deb and I had helped one another over a difficult time, and I had reason to be grateful. But gratitude's not enough, not as a basis for a permanent partnership.'

He stroked her hand. 'You didn't catch all I said, on the drive up? I didn't make myself clear?'

He pulled her to face him. 'It's you, I want, Tessa Maitland; you I've wanted since my eyes lit upon you, the day you arrived. Instantly, I knew, but the dime fully dropped when I stood watching you dancing, being touched, fondled, by another man, felt wildly, crazily jealous. I had to ask myself why this should be, though I very well knew the answer.'

His hand ran up and down her spine. 'From then on, it was an obstacle course I ran. First, I had to be sure Debra knew the score, and that took a while, though the clues had been laid long before. Then I had to wait for the mist to clear from your lovely eyes . . .'

He pulled her close, then took a glance to left and to right.

'No, not here—there are too many folk . . . Out on the balcony.'

Grasping her by the wrist, he tugged her behind him,

the way he'd done the night of the festival dance, the way
she knew he'd always do, determined, demanding, yet
protective.

The glassed-in balcony was empty of people; the
tables stood ready laid. He led her to a trellised corner,
to a wide window, and pointed through it to a full yellow
moon, a dark velvet sky, milk-white mountains.

'It's God's own country,' he murmured. 'And I go
with the territory.' The amber eyes stared yearningly
down. 'So what is it to be, Tessa Maitland? Yes, or no?'

Her heart hammered, but she wasn't going to be
rushed.

'Yes or no, what?' she asked, teasingly.

The full lips twitched. 'Yes or no, will you change your
name? Tessa Lachlan, that'd be easier for me to
remember!'

She knew a great surge of excitement, but the devil
was in her.

'Give me one good reason, why I should?' she
challenged.

'For crying out loud! Is there no pleasing you,
woman?' He sucked in breath. 'Because I admire you,
need you, want you; because I think I understand you,
and you understand me, because I love you . . . Isn't
that sufficient?'

He crushed her to him. Her body, her heart, seemed
no longer hers, but to belong to him; were his, to do as he
would, to do as she wished . . .

She smiled up. 'I guess so!' she said, and sank into his
arms.

Look out for these three great Doctor Nurse Romances coming next month

DOCTORS IN SHADOW
by Sonia Deane

When Nurse Emma Reade comes to look after Dr Simon Conway's mother and help in his practice, she realises it will be impossible to live in the same house with such a man and not fall in love. But one of the other doctors, Odile Craig, adores him — and is fiercely possessive . . .

BRIGHT CRYSTALS
by Lilian Darcy

In the French Alps Nurse Natalie Perroux meets a handsome member of the ski rescue team — and they are instantly attracted. What she doesn't foresee is the heart-rending tangle which follows the unexpected arrival of an old boyfriend from England . . .

NIGHT OF THE MOONFLOWER
by Anne Vinton

After a year's parting, physiotherapist Deborah Wyndham is at last on her way to Nigeria to join her fiancé John. But that special something seems to have gone out of their relationship, and kindly interference from the attractive Jean-Marc Roland makes things even more complicated . . .

On sale where you buy Mills & Boon romances.

The Mills & Boon rose is the rose of romance

<u>Two</u> more Doctor Nurse Romances to look out for this month

Mills & Boon Doctor Nurse Romances are proving very popular indeed. Stories range wide throughout the world of medicine — from high-technology modern hospitals to the lonely life of a nurse in a small rural community.
These are the other two titles for September.

CARIBBEAN NURSE
by Lydia Balmain
Staff Nurse Coral Summers' new job in the Caribbean is the chance of a lifetime, but couldn't she somehow have stopped herself falling in love with the arrogant surgeon Philip Kenning?

UNCERTAIN SUMMER
by Betty Neels
Nurse Serena Potts is thrilled when Dutchman Laurens van Amstel proposes to her, but the problems begin when he tries to back out of their engagement . . .

On sale where you buy Mills & Boon romances.

The Mills & Boon rose is the rose of romance

Masquerade
Historical Romances

*Intrigue
excitement
romance*

MOONSHADOW
by Valentina Luellen

To win back his family's plantation Moonshadow,
Dominic d'Estainville must marry the new owner's
daughter. Veronique agrees to the marriage, knowing
it will bring her nothing but heartbreak, for she has
loved Dominic all her life. While the American Civil
War threatens from without, Veronique battles to win
the love of a husband who despises her.

CHANCE OF LOVE
by Helen May

At the age of eighteen Miss Elinor Graham is certain
of two things. One that she will make an indifferent
school-ma'am; the other that the world can bring her
excitement and eventual security. Why then should she
proceed to fall so disastrously in love with the
impecunious Mr Christopher Brand?

Look out for these titles in your local paperback shop from
11th September 1981

ROMANCE

Variety is the spice of romance

Each month, Mills & Boon publish new romances. New stories about people falling in love. A world of variety in romance – from the best writers in the romantic world. Choose from these titles in September.

THE LION OF LA ROCHE   Yvonne Whittal
SATAN'S MASTER   Carole Mortimer
ILLUSION   Charlotte Lamb
SUBSTITUTE BRIDE   Margaret Pargeter
UNTOUCHED WIFE   Rachel Lindsay
INNOCENT OBSESSION   Anne Mather
WITCHING HOUR   Sara Craven
HILLS OF AMETHYST   Mary Moore
PASSIONATE STRANGER   Flora Kidd
MACLEAN'S WOMAN   Ann Cooper

On sale where you buy paperbacks. If you require further information or have any difficulty obtaining them, write to: Mills & Boon Reader Service, PO Box 236, Thornton Road, Croydon, Surrey CR9 3RU, England.

Mills & Boon
the rose of romance

'Everyone loves romance at Christmas'

The Mills & Boon Christmas Gift Pack is available from October 9th in the U.K. It contains four new paperback Romances from four favourite authors, in an attractive presentation case:

The Silken Cage	– Rebecca Stratton
Egyptian Honeymoon	– Elizabeth Ashton
Dangerous	– Charlotte Lamb
Freedom to Love	– Carole Mortimer

You do not pay any extra for the pack – so put it on your Christmas shopping list now.
On sale where you buy paperbacks, £3.00 (U.K. net).

The rose of romance
Mills & Boon

SAVE TIME, TROUBLE & MONEY!
By joining the exciting NEW...

Mills & Boon Romance CLUB

WITH all these EXCLUSIVE BENEFITS for every member

NOTHING TO PAY! MEMBERSHIP IS FREE TO REGULAR READERS!

IMAGINE the *pleasure* and *security* of having ALL your favourite *Mills & Boon* romantic fiction delivered right to *your* home, absolutely POST FREE... straight off the press! No waiting! No more disappointments! All this PLUS all the latest news of *new books* and *top-selling authors* in your own monthly MAGAZINE... PLUS *regular* big CASH SAVINGS... PLUS lots of wonderful strictly-limited, *members-only* SPECIAL OFFERS! All these exclusive benefits can be *yours* – right NOW – simply by joining the exciting NEW *Mills & Boon* ROMANCE CLUB. Complete and post the coupon below for FREE full-colour leaflet. It costs nothing. HURRY!

No obligation to join unless you wish!

FREE CLUB MAGAZINE Packed with *advance* news of *latest* titles and authors

Exciting offers of **FREE BOOKS** For club members ONLY

Lots of fabulous **BARGAIN OFFERS** —many at **BIG CASH SAVINGS**

FREE FULL-COLOUR LEAFLET!
CUT OUT CUT OUT COUPON BELOW AND POST IT TODAY!

To: **MILLS & BOON READER SERVICE**, P.O. Box No 236, Thornton Road, Croydon, Surrey CR9 3RU, England. WITHOUT OBLIGATION to join, please send me FREE details of the exciting NEW **Mills & Boon** ROMANCE CLUB and of all the exclusive benefits of membership.

Please write in BLOCK LETTERS below

NAME (Mrs/Miss) ....

ADDRESS ....

CITY/TOWN ....

COUNTY/COUNTRY................................. POST/ZIP CODE.................

Readers in South Africa and Zimbabwe please write to:
P.O. BOX 1872, Johannesburg, 2000. S. Africa